Wildlife *Protectors* Handbook

Wildlife *Protectors* Handbook

by Donald Heintzelman

CAPRA PRESS
SANTA BARBARA

Illustrations by Deja Hsu.
Typesetting by Stanton Publication Services, St. Paul.
Printed by McNaughton & Gunn.

LIBRARY OF CONGRESS CATALOGING-IN-PUBLICATION DATA

Heintzelman, Donald S.
  The wildlife protectors handbook / Donald Heintzelman.
    p.   cm.
  Includes bibliographical references and index.
  ISBN 0-88496-346-2 (paper) : $9.95
  1. Wildlife conservation—Handbooks, manuals, etc. 2.
Wildlife management—Handbooks, manuals, etc. 3. Wildlife
conservation—United States—Handbooks, manuals, etc. 4.
Wildlife management—United States—Handbooks, manuals, etc.
I. Title.
QL82.H35   1992
333/95' 16'0973—dc20   91-36505
                                                             CIP

CAPRA PRESS
Post Office Box 2068, Santa Barbara, CA 93120

TABLE OF CONTENTS

1

Background

W ildlife is under assault and taking a terrible beating. Hunters are blasting waterfowl into oblivion. Developers are
draining and destroying vital wetland areas needed by dozens of
species. Mourning Doves, slaughtered by the millions, decline in
population in the western United States with each hunting season.
Semi-tame White-tailed Deer are shot in parks in towns and cities
within sight of bedrooms and schoolrooms. Even graceful Tundra
Swans are killed. Above all, the human population, exploding at
an astronomical rate, increasingly stresses wild species and further
destroys their habitat.

Little wonder that the worldwide increase in endangered species
has become a torrent rushing head-on toward extinction for many
of our planet's most important and spectacular mammals, birds,
amphibians and reptiles, fishes and invertebrates.

What can we do? Everything seems so overwhelming and hope-
less. Can anything be done to deal with this crisis?

Yes! That's what this book is all about — to suggest actions that we

7

can take to protect wildlife. But first, let's put wildlife protection into perspective.

Some Historic Perspectives

Hunted, trapped, poached, poisoned, collected, sold, ignored when in desperate need, and increasingly pushed from fragmented or destroyed habitat—living space essential to its survival—countless wild species are declining in numbers. Carolina Parakeets, Great Auks, Labrador Ducks and Passenger Pigeons already are extinct. California Condors, Ivory-billed Woodpeckers, Whooping Cranes, Black-footed Ferrets and hundreds of other species are threatened or endangered. All to satisfy humankind's self-serving demands.

Within the United States, prospects for total wildlife protection seem bleak—until one examines human-wildlife relations from a four-hundred-year perspective. Perhaps some hope exists for greater protection of wildlife after all. Consider these facts:

&. During the 1600s and 1700s, almost no laws existed in colonial America to protect wildlife. Human survival was a greater concern to the colonists. Moreover, America's abundant wildlife seemed limitless—beaver, bear, bison, deer, elk, muskrats, turkeys, waterfowl and countless other birds and mammals. Laws protecting wildlife were not even contemplated in the rush to open the continent to development. Indeed, quite the opposite was true. In 1683, in Pennsylvania, hunting was allowed everywhere on the lands in William Penn's Charter. A bounty was placed on Gray Wolves. By 1721, however, Pennsylvania had adopted its first Game Law protecting White-tailed Deer from January through June.

&. By the late 1800s, slaughter of wildlife by market hunters and others reached staggering proportions. Fortunately, a few far-sighted people realized that restrictions had to be placed on the killing or no bird or beast would survive. By then, of course, the population of many species were severely reduced and others extinct.

&. By the early 1900s, concern about the survival of America's wildlife spread, and more federal and state laws were enacted to stop the killing—or at least control it. Spring waterfowl hunting was halted. Most shorebirds no longer were considered game species and hunting them was banned. The lethal plume trade, fueled by the women's hat industry, nearly exterminated egrets and herons but was halted in the nick of time, and these wonderful birds were saved. An international treaty protected most of America's migratory songbirds. The first national wildlife refuges also were established to protect certain wildlife areas. Those early refuges were inviolate in the full sense of the word; decades later many national wildlife refuges foolishly were opened to hunting and trapping. The meaning of the word refuge now is ignored.

𝕤 Still to come in this century were state and federal protection for birds of prey after years of dedicated effort by raptor conservationists, increased protection for selected other predators (after many species, such as Gray Wolves, were exterminated from much of their historic range), worldwide efforts to protect whales and dolphins, and strict state and federal laws to protect threatened and endangered species.

𝕤 Developing as a visible movement after its early 1900s beginning, the current wildlife protection movement gains more and more support yearly. Efforts to ban the use of leghold traps and all fur products continue. More ecologically sound attitudes toward wildlife and the environment are beginning to enter mainstream public thinking, as well as government wildlife policies and programs. In the mid-1970s, the animal rights movement exploded upon the scene. It continues to grow steadily, enjoying public support to the consternation of state and federal wildlife agencies that bitterly oppose it.

Collectively, these events signal important changes in human relationships with wildlife, and a steady movement toward increased wildlife protection. While important progress is being made, the process is slow and frequently frustrating. Nonetheless, much remains to be done at home and overseas. Consider these situations in other parts of the world:

𝕤 In Africa, magnificent elephants are reduced from millions to a few hundred thousand. They are endangered because of their valuable ivory tusks, and the deadly poachers who kill for jewelry. Or consider Mountain Gorillas and Chimpanzees—our cousins among animal species. As Africa's human population explodes and expands, the primates' once extensive habitat is reduced to fragmented patches of parks and reserves.

🐾 In Amazonia, and elsewhere in the tropics, the cutting and burning of rainforests are leading to massive extinction of wild species (and increased global warming).

🐾 Even Earth's most remote continent, Antarctica, is under assault. Multi-national companies and agencies of various governments are attempting to open the frigid, remote area to oil, gas, and mineral extraction. Its fabulous wildlife may soon disappear—unless current international efforts by Greenpeace and other organizations to preserve the Antarctic and its wildlife as world treasures are successful.

New Wildlife Protection Opportunities

Depressing as many of these situations are, they offer exciting new opportunities to further wildlife protection. It's important to remember, however, that all the problems will not be solved at once. A few of the difficulties facing people and wildlife include the following:

🐾 *Lyme Disease.* Since its identification in 1975 in Connecticut, Lyme disease has become one of the most widespread wildlife-associated diseases in the United States. The full scope of the problem has yet to be fully defined. Nevertheless, most medical and public health researchers conclude that killing White-tailed Deer is *not* the solution to combating the disease. Wildlife activists should be aware of this because many self-serving hunters, and some wildlife managers employed by state wildlife agencies, have attempted to use Lyme disease to justify deer hunts in urban and suburban areas. A nontechnical and comprehensive review of Lyme disease in the United States is Diana Benzaia's excellent book, *Protect Yourself from Lyme Disease* (Dell).

🐾 *Rabies.* In some eastern states, epidemics of rabies among Raccoons, Striped Skunks, and other species have caused major public concern. Make no mistake about it, human rabies is a fatal disease. However, with prompt and proper treatment few people in the United States actually die of it. But hunters, trappers, farmers, some state wildlife officials, and some public health officials use rabies to allow uncontrolled wildlife killing. Wildlife activists can counter this problem, especially in urban and suburban areas, by insisting that *all* household pets (dogs and cats), and farm animals, receive rabies inoculations.

Protecting wildlife worldwide will take vigorous work over a long time with lots of people pitching in, as well as continued professional research. Each one of us has an important role to play. Increased wildlife protection begins with you and me, at home, across cities, counties, states, nations, and around the globe. That's the key. Everything and everyone is interrelated, everyone should become involved.

Protecting wildlife in one area often affects wildlife elsewhere. A decision never to buy ivory, for example, can save individual and entire herds of elephants. It sends a strong message to citizens, business people, and governments everywhere that dead wildlife has no value. Far better they should be kept alive, allowing people to observe and appreciate, stimulating economic growth via ecotourism. Putting an emphasis on living wildlife in protected ecosystems can provide jobs for guides, tour operators, and in-services for the benefit of the local economy, as well as wildlife and ecotourists.

Not a very dramatic act, refusing to buy ivory or other wildlife products. But a boycott by hundreds of millions of people is effective! That's the key to protecting wildlife. Instead of wasting time, money and energy on actions that don't produce results, we must learn to identify what works, and then do it!

That's the purpose of this book: to provide lots of practical information for wildlife advocates to use right now. Don't look for razzle-dazzle. Protecting wildlife frequently doesn't grab headlines. But you'll know your efforts are working every time an acre of wild habitat is saved, every time fewer animals are hunted, and every time more healthy wildlife communities begin appearing.

2

Educating the Public

W ant to protect wildlife? Educate the public! Be creative! The opportunities to educate others about wildlife protection are abundant. Here are a few examples to consider. You'll surely think of others, or variations of these.

Informal Education Programs

Starting at home, and in every walk of life, even well-informed citizens can benefit from further enlightenment. Indeed, traditional conservation groups can often benefit most from an exposure to new ideas because their concept of human-wildlife relationships is often seriously distorted and obsolete. Consider the following guidelines:

🐟 **Be Informed.** Before joining any outreach program, be sure to read basic literature relating to your topic. Also try to gain firsthand experience with the program. In short, know what you are talking about! Try to attend any lectures, short courses, workshops or other informal educational opportunities available in your area. They are often excellent ways for volunteers to expand their knowledge about wildlife issues.

🐾 *Begin At Home.* There's no better place than your dining room table to discuss the environmental consequences of beef production on tropical forests, soil erosion, water pollution, and the issue of public rangeland. And don't overlook the wanton deaths of thousands of dolphins caused by some commercial tuna fishing operations.

🐾 *Visit Youth Organizations.* Extend efforts to meetings of Boy Scouts and Girl Scouts, 4-H Clubs, Boys and Girls Clubs, YM/YWCA and similar organizations. Summer camps and day care centers are also ideal places for informal wildlife programs.

🐾 *Churches and Synagogues.* Don't neglect church and synagogue gatherings. Why not present a special workshop or seminar about wildlife protection to clergy in your area? This could open their eyes and get them thinking! American religious communities are one of the most neglected groups when it comes to spreading wildlife information. I know of one church that has even organized a "fellowship" of hunters to promote hunting. Wildlife does not exist for human use; people and wildlife are all part of the web of nature. The survival of all species, including us humans, is mutually dependent.

🐾 *Conservation Organizations.* Meet with Sierra Club, Audubon Society and National Wildlife Federation members. Many are not opposed to hunting and consider the entire "hunting issue" a minor one compared to the worldwide loss of wildlife habitat and biodiversity, global warming and the greenhouse effect. Regretfully, many bird watchers are almost as hostile to the concept of wildlife protection as are hunters and trappers.

🐾 *Senior Citizen Organizations.* All across America these organizations conduct a wide variety of regularly scheduled activities. Millions of retired people participate. It is unlikely that many of these organizations devote much time to wildlife issues, and that provides wildlife advocates with outstanding opportunities to advance the cause of wildlife protection. Senior citizens have a lifetime of work experience and a wide range of occupational skills, which can be extremely valuable when applied to wildlife projects.

🐾 *Social Service Organizations.* Most social service organizations are extremely people- and tradition-oriented because they primarily serve human needs, often the poor, hungry or homeless. It is important that skilled activists discuss the need for increased wildlife protection with leaders of social service organizations. The Safari Club International tried to secure cooperation for its "Hunters Against Hunger" project from organizations such as the Salvation Army. In "Hunters Against Hunger," hunters were to donate some of their kill to help feed those receiving meals from social service agencies. Alert activists need to fully inform social service officials so that they understand the ecological and wildlife implications of cooperating with such a program.

🐾 *Sportsmen Organizations.* Activists who are articulate and well-prepared should make presentations to rod and gun clubs. Expect hostility from these people, but remember that hunters represent only 9% of the American adult population. Each convert to wildlife protection from this crowd means one less hunter or trapper, and fewer animals killed!

Formal Educational Activities

Educational courses and workshops, sometimes providing certification or graduate level (master's degree) credit for public school teachers, are essential components of wildlife protection educational efforts. Remember, by reaching teachers one indirectly reaches thousands of children on a continuing basis. Trained teachers who become wildlife advocates play a particularly important role in public education. The following examples of courses and workshops should be considered:

🐾 *Public and Private Schools.* Work on developing in-service teacher training classes, workshops (perhaps for salary or academic credit), presentations, or teaching units for children in grades K-12 within specific school districts. Many states and school districts already have environmental programs included in their requirements, but much more emphasis is needed on wildlife conservation. It also is important that selection of wildlife information be as broad as possible to reflect worldwide relationships and issues—even for children at the most elemental level.

For example, if protection of tropical rainforests is the topic, children between ages three to seven will enjoy using an excellent and inexpensive coloring book entitled *Color The Rainforest* as a useful introduction to this issue. Older children also can benefit from reading *The Rainforest Book* (Living Planet Press) and many other excellent books dealing with this vital issue.

🐾 **Intermediate Units.** From time to time, in cooperation with intermediate units in Pennsylvania (regional educational agencies under the Pennsylvania Department of Education), the Wildlife Information Center offers in-service courses and workshops for teachers needing additional credits for certification. The course or workshop topics include hawk watching, urban wildlife, world wildlife conservation, and raptor biology, conservation and ecology. The one credit (15 contact hours) world wildlife conservation course, for example, includes detailed discussions and slide programs dealing with wildlife issues in Pennsylvania and the United States, the Galapagos Islands, Amazonia and the West Indies, East Africa, and the Antarctic and Falkland Islands.

Although teacher certification requirements vary from state to state, wildlife supporters should investigate opportunities in their state to prepare and offer special wildlife courses for teachers. By doing so they will be getting wildlife protection information into the mainstream educational process.

🐾 **College and University Seminars.** At the university and especially community college level, it sometimes is possible to offer special seminars on nontraditional topics, such as wildlife protection. Some may be noncredit courses open to the general public, while others may offer one to three undergraduate college credits.

🐾 **College Intern Programs.** College intern programs, now used by many wildlife conservation organizations, provide undergraduates with excellent opportunities to assist professionals and thereby gain valuable, practical experience. Students interested in intern programs can seek further information from appropriate professors or college placement offices at the institution they attend. Some wildlife and environmental magazines also list intern opportunities. If all else fails, simply write to the President or Executive Director of an organization that interests you and inquire if they offer (or would establish) an intern program. The National Wildlife Federation's (1400 Sixteenth St., NW, Washington, DC 20036–2266) annual *Conservation Directory* provides names and addresses of hundreds of wildlife and conservation organizations in the United States. Ask your college librarian for a copy. However, keep in mind that many groups included in that directory do not oppose hunting, and some strongly support it. Read the descriptions of the organizations carefully, and select only those that work to eliminate hunting, trapping and to increase wildlife protection. The *Animal Organizations & Services Directory* (Animal Stories, 16783 Beach Blvd., Suite 214-F, Huntington Beach, CA 92647) is a similar source for names and addresses of wildlife, humane and animal rights organizations.

Commemorative Events

Wildlife advocates have the benefit of a variety of public events designed to focus attention on specific wildlife issues. Here are some effective events held worldwide or in the United States:

&. *Earth Day 1990.* Promoted as a commemoration of the need to foster new, effective ways to protect the earth from environmental destruction, and as an extension of the original 1970 celebration, Earth Day 1990 enlisted the active participation of approximately 120 million people worldwide. Countless communities in the United States had Earth Day celebrations. However, advocates of wildlife protection were disappointed by the lack of attention about the needs of wildlife, the biodiversity crisis, and the short memory exhibited by the general public after the event. Nevertheless, Earth Day celebrations still represent the single largest concentrations of public support for environmental protection. As such, they demonstrate that commemorative events can bring together huge numbers of people and focus their attention on important issues for short periods of time. That's a start. However, much organized follow-up is required if the initial awareness is to become a continuing body of support for wildlife and environmental protection.

🐦 *National Bald Eagle Day.* Unknown to most people, in 1982 Congress passed a resolution to establish National Bald Eagle Day. Regretfully, what should have been a national celebration of our spectacular national bird went unnoticed by most people including most wildlife activists. Nevertheless, the opportunity was there for those who were aware.

🐦 *National Birds of Prey Conservation Week.* In 1984, Congress enacted legislation for National Birds of Prey Conservation Week. Its purpose was to focus the American public's attention on the continuing need for the protection of birds of prey and their habitats. Fortunately, it received much wider publicity than the earlier 1982 National Bald Eagle Day. Some states, such as Alaska, made good use of the event, as did the Tennessee Valley Authority, which issued a spectacular color poster nationwide. Regretfully, most animal rights activists, bird watchers, hawk watchers and wildlife protectors failed (or, in some cases, refused) to participate. That's tragic and foolish. They let slip away a marvelous opportunity to promote wildlife protection on a national scale. Hopefully, as similar events come up in the future, everyone concerned with wildlife protection will demonstrate more imagination and take full advantage of the opportunities!

🐦 *State Hawk Watching Weeks.* During the past 10 years or more, governors of various states have issued proclamations for Hawk Watching Weeks. The general intent of these events is similar to that of National Birds of Prey Conservation Week, namely to promote greater public awareness and concern for raptor conservation. In 1980, the Governor of Arkansas also issued a proclamation for Eagle Awareness Week to focus increased public attention on Bald Eagles.

Most commemorative events for wildlife promote life and the

preservation of habitat. However, the annual White House proclamation of National Hunting and Fishing Day is designed to promote the killing of wildlife. Several recent Presidents endorsed National Hunting and Fishing Day and are themselves hunters, which indicates how distant the idea of wildlife protection is from the serious consideration of our highest elected public official. Nevertheless, opportunities can be seized to promote wildlife protection, even during National Hunting and Fishing Day. Consider the following:

• *Public Demonstrations.* Wildlife advocates sometimes hold public demonstrations to oppose National Hunting and Fishing Day and to draw attention to the destructive problems caused by hunting and game management. Public demonstrations are primarily media events designed to reach as wide an audience as possible with wildlife protection messages. Generally, demonstrations do not have an immediate impact upon the policies of state or federal wildlife agencies. I know of no evidence that agency policies are being altered by public demonstrations created by wildlife advocates. However, some developments suggest that hunters, hunting organizations, state and federal wildlife agencies, and other such "establishment" organizations are becoming increasingly sensitive to anti-hunting activities like public demonstrations. For example, the December 1990 issue of *Ornithological Newsletter* published by the Ornithological Societies of North America contained a news item reporting that representatives of more than 125 agriculture, biomedical, conservation, industry, outdoor media and sportsmen organizations recently established a national organization whose purpose is to "support responsible resource management and campaign against animal rights extremism." The notice further stated that "strident activism is interfering with the rights of sportsmen to hunt and fish, hampering food and fiber production, and disrupting medical research to protect human life." Interestingly, the new organization's interim chairman was an official of the Wildlife Management Institute, a pro-hunting organization.

• *Literature Distribution.* Activists can distribute literature demonstrating the bias of state and federal wildlife programs. Appropriate information can be prepared especially for this use or secured from other organizations. Distribution of this type of literature usually is done by volunteers manning outreach tables at public events.

• **Representation on Government Commissions.** Emphasis also can be placed on having women and minority groups represented on governmental wildlife agency commissions and staffs. In Pennsylvania, for instance, the Game Commission is composed of aging, white, male hunters. Thus, the views of women, minority segments of society, and anti-hunters never are represented during Game Commission meetings. Similar situations exist in most other states, and within the U.S. Fish and Wildlife Service. Therefore, it is important that wildlife advocates actively seek representation on governmental wildlife agencies, at least at the state level. It will probably be much more difficult to do so within the U.S. Fish and Wildlife Service.

Conferences

Wildlife conferences on a wide assortment of topics now are held across the country and internationally, offering wildlife advocates excellent opportunities to meet experts. Biodiversity, raptors and wildlife fertility control are a few of the important topics featured at these conferences.

If an organization has the resources and experts available, they can host their own conferences. In January 1987, for example, the Wildlife Information Center held "Pennsylvania Raptor Conference 1987: Raptors and Public Education" which 300 people attended from the eastern United States. Roger Tory Peterson, the world's foremost ornithologist, was the keynote speaker, and 15 other speakers made outstanding presentations on a wide range of educational topics regarding raptors. No previous conference had addressed the subject of raptors and public education in such a comprehensive manner.

Similarly, in Philadelphia in 1988, PNC (an animal rights think tank) sponsored the world's first international conference devoted to wildlife contraception. Wildlife biologists presented state-of-the-art information on the development and use of wildlife fertility control techniques in many parts of the world. In 1990, a second such conference was held in Australia and updated information was presented.

Note that small organizations with limited funds took the lead in developing both the 1987 raptor and the 1988 wildlife contraception conferences. However, at a certain point, the resources of major organizations such as The Humane Society of the United States are necessary to provide the essential push to achieve the use of techniques such as wildlife fertility control in appropriate locations. Therefore, close cooperation is important between small and large organizations working on specific wildlife issues. Each has its own important role to play.

Meeting the Media

Using the media to spread information to the public is an essential of wildlife activism. That's particularly true because most newspaper outdoor editors and writers are hunters and fill their columns with pro-hunting information. Thus wildlife information in newspapers is usually very biased toward hunting and game management rather than toward sound ecology and conservation biology. Overcoming this editorial bias is extremely difficult. However, here are some ways that alternative views can be published in newspapers:

&. *Letters-to-Editors.* The importance of letters to newspaper and magazine editors can't be stressed too strongly. Readers' letters in daily newspapers are among the most regularly read features. They allow anyone to print a viewpoint quickly and without cost. If you want to promote wildlife protection, there is no better means than writing letters to editors. They should be written much more regularly by all activists.

Put the focus on the distorted, pro-hunting propaganda routinely provided to millions of readers. It's mostly misinformation designed to spread public support for sport hunting. Use hard-hitting, accurate, ecologically sound information and alternative viewpoints. Also meet with editors to seek accurate wildlife protection coverage.

☙ **Newspaper Columns.** Some newspaper editors may be willing to allow wildlife supporters to write regular columns on wildlife protection. The Wildlife Information Center, for example, has for several years produced a monthly column for a weekly newspaper in eastern Pennsylvania. Payment for these columns may or may not be provided, but a writer can seek $10 to $15 per column to defray the cost of research and preparation.

☙ **News Releases.** News releases are one of the most common ways to get wildlife information to the media. Their careful use is strongly recommended, even though many never find their way into print. They are inexpensive to produce and can be carefully edited before distribution to the media. Send copies to daily and weekly newspapers, local shopping guides, and radio, television and cable stations. If the topic has broad appeal, send copies to major wire services including the Associated Press and United Press International.

When preparing news releases keep them brief (preferably one page), include an arresting headline, and don't forget to provide essential details regarding what, when, who, where and why. Also be sure to include the name and telephone number of a contact person so reporters can get additional information. The following sample news release from the Wildlife Information Center is typical of those we issue:

WILDLIFE NEWS RELEASE

Wildlife Information Center, Inc. 629 Green St. Allentown, PA 18102 (215) 434–1637
For Release May 21, 1990 Contact Donald S. Heintzelman (215) 434–1637

Wildlife Center Urges Complete
Ban on Outdoor Balloon Releases

With countless outdoor activities either scheduled or forthcoming this spring and summer, outdoor releases of colorful balloons to celebrate events is a popular activity. Unfortunately, this seemingly harmless activity also is lethal to marine wildlife such as sea turtles, dolphins, whales, and seabirds such as albatrosses.

Therefore, the Wildlife Information Center, a national wildlife conservation organization based in Allentown, PA, is calling to the public's attention the following basic facts regarding this wildlife and environmental issue.

🐌 Balloons drifting into the ocean are increasingly mistaken for food by sea turtles, dolphins and whales. Balloons also are lethal to albatrosses and other seabirds.

🐌 After being ingested by marine life, balloons either choke them to death or cause major intestinal blockages leading to death of the victim. At least one human infant also choked to death after swallowing a balloon.

🐌 Release of balloons into the atmosphere represents a needless source of ocean and terrestrial pollution.

🐌 Balloons landing on fields, in forests and in wetlands also represent needless landscape and wildlife habitat litter.

🐌 Certain metallic types of balloons also have caused electrical power failures after landing on power lines. Electrical utility companies are becoming increasingly concerned about this problem.

🐌 Release of balloons into the atmosphere continues to instill in people the idea that resources are limitless and can be endlessly discarded without environmental impact.

🐌 Even when numerous organizations release only small numbers of balloons, the collective total is considerable and continues to represent a threat to marine wildlife.

Therefore, the Wildlife Information Center again is issuing its annual appeal to organizations requesting that there be no outdoor releases of balloons.

Balloons are colorful and delightful to watch. However, if they are used, they should always be tied down. Similarly, children should be urged not to release them.

In short, enjoy them—but don't release them!

-WIC-

🐾 *Press Conferences.* When wildlife advocates have exceptionally important and timely information for the public, a press conference is justified. As a matter of professional courtesy, representatives of all newspaper, radio and television stations in the area should be invited to the conference. Keep in mind, however, that many will not attend unless the story is sufficiently compelling.

Where the conference is held is determined by who is calling the conference or other circumstances linked with the story to be released. Generally, as a matter of convenience, some central location should be selected. If the story relates to a site of exceptional importance to wildlife, the conference could be held there. Provide the media with accurate directions for reaching the location, and make sure an attractive or dramatic site is selected for the benefit of news photographers and television camera crews.

At such meetings with the media, prepared statements usually are made first, followed by questions and answers. In addition, printed copies of all formal statements, news releases and other materials should be assembled into information packets and passed out to all media representatives attending. Be sure to save several copies for future reference.

In addition, special audio and/or videotape packets can be prepared for media representatives. Be prepared for short interviews with radio and television crews, and newspaper reporters as well.

The hour that a press conference is held determines which segment of the media has the first opportunity to use the information. For example, if you want the information on the evening news, the conference can be held in early afternoon. Meeting an afternoon newspaper deadline generally is not a consideration since there are so few.

🐾 *Public Service Ads.* Use of free public service ads in local publications is an innovative but seldom used method. The Wildlife

Information Center occasionally uses them in cooperating Pennsylvania newspapers. Here are the texts of our most popular public service ads:

Bald Eagle/America's National Bird. For more than two centuries, the Bald Eagle has been America's national bird—our symbol of freedom. Like all birds of prey, or raptors, it is one of nature's most beautiful and ecologically important birds. Once they were slaughtered, then endangered by DDT pollution. Today eagles, and all birds of prey, are protected. And recovering from DDT pollution. Yet some still are shot illegally. Please don't shoot these magnificent birds! For more information about Bald Eagles, and birds of prey protection, write to "Eagles" at the Wildlife Information Center, 629 Green St., Allentown, PA 18102. Or call (215) 434-1637 and leave your full name, address, and telephone number if an answering machine comes on. Keep Birds of Prey Flying! Presented as a public service by [name of newspaper]

Birds of Prey/Masters of the Sky. Birds of prey, or raptors, are among nature's most beautiful and ecologically important birds. Once large numbers were slaughtered. Today all birds of prey are protected. Yet some still are shot illegally. Please don't shoot these masters of the sky! For more information about birds of prey protection, write to "Raptors" at the Wildlife Information Center, 629 Green St., Allentown, PA 18102. Or call (215) 434-1637 and leave your full name, address, and telephone number if an answering machine comes on. Keep Hawks and Owls Flying! Presented as a public service by [name of newspaper]

White-tailed Deer/They Also Need A Home. White-tailed Deer. These graceful animals are our most widely distributed, large native mammals. However, habitat loss forces some to live in smaller and smaller natural areas. Deer can even venture into cities. And many are killed in collisions with vehicles along highways. Please help to protect deer and all wildlife by working to save its habitat! For more information about habitat protection, write to "Habitat" at the Wildlife Information Center, 629 Green St., Allentown, PA 18102. Or call (215) 434–1637 and leave your full name, address, and telephone number if an answering machine comes on. Protect Wildlife. Save Habitat! Presented as a public service by [name of newspaper]

Habitat/It's Wildlife's Home, Too. Bogs. Caves. Deserts. Fields. Forests. Marshes. Meadows. Oceans. Rainforests. Seas. Swamps. Tundra. Wetlands. Woodlots. Earth's priceless wildlife heritage lives in many places (habitats). But habitat loss threatens more and more species with extinction. Please help to protect wildlife and its vital habitat! For more information about habitat protection, write to "Habitat" at the Wildlife Information Center, 629 Green St., Allentown, PA 18102. Or call (215) 434–1637 and leave your full name, address, and telephone number if an answering machine comes on. Protect Wildlife Habitat! Presented as a public service by [name of newspaper].

🐾 **Public Service Announcements.** Use of free public service ads on radio or television provides additional educational opportunities. The ads should be 15, 30, or 60 seconds in length. Remember that most radio and television stations will not use public service ads they deem controversial. So don't expect anti-fur or anti-hunting public service ads to be broadcast except under the most unusual or exceptional circumstances. However, here's some possible wildlife protection topics:

• Appeals to the public to help save and protect wildlife habitat.

• Suggestions for avoiding deer-vehicle collisions.

• Suggestions for improving wildlife habitat such as planting shrubs, trees and wildflowers.

• Suggestions for altering one's diet to aid wildlife protection (avoiding consumption of meat and poultry).

• Suggestions for using bird feeders and bird houses.

Here are three typical public service ads (PSAs) provided to radio stations by the Wildlife Information Center. Feel free to send these to your local radio stations. Since radio stations receive large numbers of PSAs, most of which are never used, it is best to telephone radio station PSA directors a few days after mailing your PSAs to discuss them and encourage their broadcast. Even if a particular PSA is not used, you have established a contact with the station that can be useful in the future. However, don't be surprised if most stations will not broadcast anti-hunting or anti-fur PSAs. Generally, it's better to focus your messages on important, non-controversial issues that already are provided for via laws or regulations, such as birds of prey protection.

Birds of Prey Protection

10 Seconds:

Birds of prey are important members of wildlife communities.

All are protected.

Please don't shoot them.

A public service message from the Wildlife Information Center, Inc., Allentown, PA.

20 Seconds:

Birds of prey, or raptors, include eagles, hawks, falcons, owls, and even vultures.

They are important members of wildlife communities.

All are legally protected.

Please don't shoot birds of prey.

A public service message from the Wildlife Information Center, Inc., Allentown, PA.

30 Seconds:
    Birds of prey, or raptors, are among nature's most beautiful and ecologically important birds.
    They include eagles, hawks, falcons, owls, and even vultures.
    Once large numbers were slaughtered.
    Today all birds of prey are protected.
    Yet some still are shot illegally.
    Please don't shoot birds of prey.
    They are necessary members of wildlife communities.
    A public service message from the Wildlife Information Center, Inc., Allentown, PA.

⚙ Radio and Television. Radio and television are as important as newspapers in disseminating wildlife protection information. Generally, the same media techniques used in contacting newspapers also apply to the electronic media. However, if interviews are granted, the few seconds of air time permits the use of only the most essential information. So choose your words carefully.

In addition, when dealing with television it is usually helpful to have available either 35mm color slides or 1/2 inch or 3/4 inch videotape footage of the subject of your news story. Keep all originals for your files, providing extra or duplicate slides or videotape to the station. Sometimes, original slides or tape can be taken to the station where they can duplicate what they need and immediately return the originals to you. Finally, you should require on-screen title credits for any of your slides or videotape they broadcast.

Project WILD

One wildlife educational product widely used in public and private schools in the United States is a program called Project WILD, developed by pro-hunting western states wildlife agencies. While many sections of this program are worthwhile, some parts have been attacked for their pro-hunting bias by such organizations as The Humane Society of the United States, Friends of Animals, Fund for Animals, and other animal rights organizations.

The issue is complicated further by state wildlife agencies' avid endorsement of Project WILD in public schools. In Pennsylvania, for example, the Pennsylvania Game Commission printed a misleading statement in its monthly magazine *Pennsylvania Game News* claiming that the Pennsylvania Department of Education endorsed Project WILD for public school use. However, after investigation by the Wildlife Information Center, the Pennsylvania Secretary of Education wrote a letter that the Department of Education does *not* endorse Project WILD (or any other specific curriculum) for use in Pennsylvania's schools.

Other flaws in Project WILD materials are detailed in two booklets entitled *The Dangers of Project WILD* and *A Humane Teaching Guide for Project WILD* (The Humane Society of the United States).

Speaking For Wildlife

In addition to the many useful educational opportunities already discussed, the Wildlife Information Center, Friends of Animals, Fund For Animals and The Humane Society of the United States offer or recommend the expanded use of the following:

🐾 *Bumperstickers.* Many animal rights and wildlife conservation organizations sell bumperstickers that cover a wide range of issues. They provide an inexpensive and effective means of promoting the wildlife cause.

🐾 *Computer Software.* In view of the popularity of personal computers, it is surprising that so little software has been developed to aid in wildlife protection. The Wildlife Information Center is working to improve that situation. In 1990, it released a Hyper-Card shareware stack (requiring HyperCard version 1.2 or higher) for use on Macintosh computers. Called "Wildlife Protector," it is a pioneering effort to provide basic wildlife information to high school, college, and university students. Wildlife activists will find "Wildlife Protector" equally useful.

The stack is organized into seven sections: (1) About the Wildlife Information Center, Inc., (2) CITES, (3) Endangered Species, (4) Hunting, (5) Laws and Enforcement, (6) Reading List, and (7) Wildlife including deer, raptors and various issues.

Information included in the endangered species section, for example, lists through April 15, 1990, all federally threatened or endangered mammals, birds, reptiles, amphibians and fishes found within the United States and its territories. The section dealing with laws and enforcement includes the addresses of federal wildlife law enforcement offices, similar information by state, and those for U.S. territories. Students also will find the seventeen-part reading list especially valuable when preparing term papers because it includes key book references for animal rights, the Antarctic, biological diversity, birds of prey, conservation, endangered species and extinction, predators and predation, tropical forests, whales and dolphins, wildlife protection, wolves and more.

The shareware stack is copyrighted by the Wildlife Information Center, which reserves all rights to it. For a nominal fee, Apple Macintosh computer users may buy the stack and make copies for associates, friends, organizations and others. However, the Center asks that people register their copies with the Wildlife Information Center. There are important benefits for doing so: (1) they will receive one free update upon release of the next available version, (2) they will receive a one-year membership (which includes our publications) in the Wildlife Information Center if they are not already a member, and (3) their financial support will help the Center continue its wildlife protection work.

The appropriate registration fee as outlined below, payable in U.S. dollars, is modest. All registrations should be mailed to the Wildlife Information Center, Inc., 629 Green St., Allentown, PA 18102. Written confirmation of receipt of each registration will be provided.

[ ] Current WIC Members /Includes Disk & One Update
@ $15.00
[ ] Non-WIC Member/Disk, One Update, & WIC Membership
@ $25.00
[ ] Business, Corporate,& Governmental Agency
@ $35.00
    (and all orders outside the U.S.A.)

The Wildlife Information Center expects to produce additional shareware database stacks in the future. Several are in the planning or preparation stage.

🐾 **Exhibit Display Units.** Many organizations also use indoor display units featuring color photographs, appropriate labels and signs, and handout literature on various wildlife protection issues. The display unit used by the Wildlife Information Center, for example, usually features historic and current photographs illustrating the evolution of public attitudes and legislation from the days of hawk shooting to current hawk protection, and related educational and hawk watching activities at former hawk shooting sites, such as Bake Oven Knob and Hawk Mountain in eastern Pennsylvania. Additional panels of the exhibit feature photographs of endangered species, photographs of deer-vehicle collisions, a sample Swareflex roadside reflector for reducing deer roadkills, photographs of attractive wildlife habitat and a donation canister for the Center's wildlife refuge land purchase fund.

This same unit also can be rearranged using available photographs and labels to focus attention on other such as tropical forests, the fight to save the Antarctic, or any other topic we wish to feature. Thus, with proper planning, indoor exhibit display units offer effective opportunities to educate the general public and special interest groups at meetings, conferences or other events. The exhibits also can be used at public hearings to influence legislators and the media covering the hearings. The Humane Society of the United States did this at a major public hearing in Pennsylvania on legislation prohibiting the import and sale of wild birds as pets. Color photographs vividly illustrated the serious problems caused by international traffic in live wild birds. The cost of a moderately sized unit and the preparation of necessary photographs and signs is approximately $1,000. Since display units are used repeatedly, the investment is money well spent as it lends a professional appearance to an organization's presentation.

🐾 **Give A Wildlife Book Program.** Donating wildlife and ecology books to libraries is another way to spread the word. The Wildlife Information Center, for example, operates an informal "Give A Wildlife Book" program and has donated dozens of wildlife and ecology books to a score of libraries in eastern Pennsylvania. Libraries receiving the books insert donor bookplates so readers can see that our organization made the donation. This is one way individuals and small organizations can quickly help advance public education about wildlife protection.

Selecting books for donation to libraries can be confusing to people unfamiliar with wildlife literature. However, the Wildlife Information Center annually reviews hundreds of books in the "Wildlife Book Review" section of its *Wildlife Activist* newsletter. For activists, there is no better summary of newly published wildlife and ecology books. Among books to consider for donation are:

• *Field Identification Guides.* Field identification guides for wildlife are among the most basic and important books that can be donated to libraries. The Peterson Field Guide series (Houghton Mifflin) and the various Golden nature guides (Golden Press) are especially recommended. Other excellent field guides from other publishers also exist.

• *Ecology Books.* Books that provide nontechnical introductions to wildlife ecology also are important.

• *Specific Species Books.* Excellent books frequently appear studying the life history and ecology of specific species. Some are suitable for donation to libraries.

• *Regional Books.* Books about specific regions should be considered for donation to libraries. For example, excellent books are available dealing with tropical and temperate rainforests, the Antarctic, the Arctic, and many other areas.

🐾 *Outreach Tables.* Use of outreach tables at shopping malls, community fairs and similar events is a popular means of speaking for wildlife while raising funds for wildlife protection organizations. Volunteers usually staff these tables, distribute free or inexpensive literature on wildlife issues, and sell other wildlife-related items such as books, bumperstickers, notecards and T-shirts. A donation canister or two also should be present. Volunteers usually encourage passers-by to join the organization sponsoring the table. That's important. Members provide financial support!

🐾 *Speakers Bureau.* Many organizations, including local service clubs, regularly need short (15 to 20 minute) programs for their meetings. Filling that need is always a problem, particularly if they have no money to pay for speakers. This provides excellent opportunities for speakers bureau volunteers to present wildlife protection programs. Good topics include the need to preserve biodiversity, loss of temperate and tropical rainforests, hunting, trapping, the use of fur, impacts of land development on wildlife and the environment, proposed commercial exploitation of Antarctic resources and its wildlife, flaws in game management, and problems with governmental wildlife policies and programs. Some organizations have packaged programs available for a modest cost. Alternatively, organizations can recruit the assistance of local photographers and writers to prepare original programs slanted to local issues.

&. *Postage and Other Stamps.* Postage stamps, by attracting the attention of millions to bird and wildlife species, are most important. Wildlife featured on U.S. stamps during recent years include the state birds of all 50 states, owls, whales and dolphins. When wildlife stamps are available, activists should use them. Every time a person unfamiliar with wildlife notices one of these stamps, we have a potential recruit to the roster of wildlife enthusiasts.

Many foreign nations feature wildlife on their postage stamps, which are a source of national pride and important revenue. That's particularly true for many third world nations in Africa, South America and the West Indies. When collectors buy these stamps, they indirectly help to save foreign wildlife.

Various organizations also release wildlife stamps as a means of fund raising annually. These stamps are extremely successful in attracting members and support. Activists, however, should be aware that some groups issuing wildlife stamps (such as the National Wildlife Federation) are pro-hunting organizations. Others, such as the National Audubon Society, are not strictly pro-hunting but they have not opposed it when they should have, as in the cases of the Mourning Dove, Sandhill Crane and Tundra Swan.

Books and Articles

Activists with exceptional knowledge about wildlife protection, who have good references and who write well, may wish to submit newspaper or magazine articles, or even book length manuscripts, about various aspects of the subject. The idea for the preparation of this book, for example, sprang from an examination of two Living Planet Press books—*The Animal Rights Handbook* and *The Rainforest Book*—and the realization that there was no similar book specifically about wildlife protection.

How and Where to Find Additional Information

For more information than is provided in this book, look in a school or public library. If you live near a college or university, perhaps you can use their collections. The following are good reference sources:

Standard Encyclopedias. Standard references almost always contain excellent sections on specific wildlife species, as well as broader topics. In many cases, the information in these books is all you will need.

Special Encyclopedias. Special encyclopedias devoted to specific animal groups are available in some library collections. The following are recommended:

Grzimek, Bernhard (Editor). *Grzimek's Animal Life Encyclopedia.* 13 vols. Van Nostrand Reinhold, 1972.

Encyclopedia of the Animal World. 12 vols. Facts On File, 1989.

Special Dictionaries. Special dictionaries also provide helpful information on various families of animals. For birds, I recommend the following:

Campbell, Bruce and Elizabeth Lack. *A Dictionary of Birds.* Buteo Books, 1985.

Terres, John K. *The Audubon Society Encyclopedia of North American Birds.* Alfred A. Knopf, 1980.

Thomson, A. Landsborough. *A New Dictionary of Birds.* McGraw-Hill, 1964.

&. *Magazines.* Many periodicals discuss wildlife. Among the best are *Animals' Agenda, E Magazine, National Geographic, Natural History, Smithsonian* and *Wildlife Conservation.* Many wildlife organizations also publish magazines such as *Audubon* or *National Wildlife.* Some may be in your library. However, keep in mind that some do not oppose hunting and trapping.

&. *Wildlife Protection Books.* I hope you are opposed to hunting and trapping, and recommend reading the following books for additional information on this subject:

Amory, Cleveland. *Man Kind? Our Incredible War on Wildlife.* Harper & Row, 1974.

Baker, Ron. *The American Hunting Myth.* Vantage Press, 1985.

Scheffer, Victor B. *A Voice For Wildlife.* Charles Scribner's Sons, 1974.

Wildlife Field Trips

Taking people on field trips to local parks, or farther afield to wildlands areas, are among the most enjoyable ways of introducing people to the wonders of wildlife. Bird watchers long have been aware of this and as a group spend more time in the field observing and photographing wildlife than any other segment of American society. Among locations suitable for field trips are:

&. *National Parks.* National parks and monuments are ideal areas for wildlife field trips. Many parks have professional naturalists who lead nature walks, present semi-formal programs, and gladly answer questions. Stop at park visitor centers, ask for information, and secure free or inexpensive handout literature such as checklists of birds and other wildlife in the park.

&. *National Wildlife Refuges.* Although many problems beset the operation of our national wildlife refuges, not the least of which is the hunting allowed on many of them, these areas still are among the nation's most interesting wildlife areas. Most offer outstanding field trips and photographic opportunities.

🐾 *State Parks.* State parks abound in the United States. Those that preserve wildlands, wetlands and other important habitats provide activists with excellent locations for field trips. Many state parks also have park ranger programs, visitor centers and a selection of free literature. Regretfully, more and more state parks are being opened to hunting, and wildlife advocates increasingly are protesting hunting in state parks. For example, in 1988, the Wildlife Information Center published a detailed examination of White-tailed Deer hunts in Tyler State Park near Philadelphia. Activists have held dozens of public protests against deer hunts at other state parks in Pennsylvania and elsewhere. Despite these inappropriate hunting liberties, many state parks still offer excellent field trip opportunities.

🐾 *County and Local Parks.* Productive wildlife field trips also can be taken in many county and local parks, even those in major American cities. Good sources of information about these opportunities are available at local nature centers.

🐾 *Private Wildlife Refuges.* One can enjoy fine field trips in private wildlife refuges. Generally, activity in these sites is strictly regulated to assure the safety of the wildlife and their habitat. Some private refuges have paid professional staffs and offer nature walks or field trips. Inquire at a the refuge office for further information.

Many books offer valuable assistance in helping plan, organize and conduct wildlife field trips. Two books by Joseph Bharat Cornell are particularly helpful in introducing children to the wonders of nature—*Sharing Nature With Children* (Ananda Publications) and *Listening to Nature/How to Deepen Your Awareness of Nature* (Dawn Publications). John W. Brainerd's *The Nature Observer's Handbook* (Globe Pequot Press) also is useful.

Numerous guides to bird finding contain details and directions for visiting locations where wild birds flourish. In addition, *The Audubon Society Field Guide to Natural Places* (Pantheon Books) contains much useful information about northeast and mid-Atlantic coastal and inland areas. Check with your local book shops and libraries.

3

Economic Power

M oney talks. That's true in business, politics and wildlife protection. It's high time wildlife advocates recognize this fundamental fact! There is no more effective way to further wildlife protection than to demonstrate that living wildlife can provide major economic benefits to people, communities and governments.

Hunters and trappers long ago recognized the advantages of promoting the economic worth of their activities. They spend hundreds of millions of dollars annually to kill wildlife in the name of sport, and they make sure that business, industry and government officials are fully informed of that fact. That's why state and federal wildlife agencies are dominated by pro-hunting administrators, and why many laws and regulations support hunters' and trappers' demands rather than wildlife protection. A summary of the economic value of consumptive wildlife uses is provided in *Valuing Wildlife* edited by Daniel J. Decker and Gary R. Goff (Westview Books).

Make no mistake about it. If wildlife fails to pay its way alive, it will do so in a rifle sight. Dead. Wildlife definitely has economic power, but so far, the economic balance has been in favor of killing. Wildlife activists face a challenge to reverse this statistic and advocate a new balance. It needs to be done in the United States, and certainly in the third world where some of the world's most spectacular wildlife groups still survive.

Here are some dollar and cents statistics reported in the *1985 National Survey of Fishing, Hunting, and Wildlife Associated Recreation* published by the U.S. Fish and Wildlife Service:

🐾 16.7 million adult hunters in the United States spent a total of $41.4 billion on hunting-related activities. A lot of money for killing wildlife!

🐾 Nine percent of these hunters were women. In the entire American population, 18% of males were hunters, and 2% of women.

🐾 96% of hunters were white, 3% black, and 1% from other races.

🐾 There were 134.7 million adult wildlife users who spent a total of $14.3 billion on nonlethal wildlife activities. As much as that seems, it is much less than the amount spent by hunters.

🐾 Nonconsumptive adult wildlife users also spent more than $3.6 billion on the equipment necessary for their activities. These included field guides, binoculars, spotting scopes, photographic film and developing, photographic equipment, day packs, outdoor clothing, bird seed, nest boxes, bird houses, feeders and bird baths. That's an average of $177 per person.

🐾 54% of men and 46% of women participated in primary, residential, nonconsumptive wildlife-related activities.

🐾 Among adults, primary, residential, nonconsumptive wildlife users 92% are white, 6% are black, and 2% represent other races.

Even though non-killing wildlife users generate impressive sums for numerous businesses and industries, hunters spend much more. It's time that wildlife advocates begin putting significant effort and money into key requirements of wildlife protection. Here are some opportunities where activists may want to increase their spending:

🐾 Saving land as wildlife refuges. Without habitat, wildlife cannot survive. That means raising money for the purchase of land as inviolate refuges. The Wildlife Information Center, for example, decided to campaign in 1990 for a wildlife refuge land fund and raised more than $21,000 toward this vital effort.

🐾 Supporting innovative wildlife protection organizations.

🐾 Systematically building changes in public attitudes and governmental wildlife policies.

🐾 Educating children, adults, government officials, business and industry officials, and nonprofit foundation officials to modify traditional attitudes toward the relationship between people, wildlife and nature.

In short, why allow hunters and trappers to use economic arguments to promote their lethal and ecologically unsound activities? Why allow them to claim that they alone pay for wildlife conservation when they actually pay to kill and alter wildlife habitats to benefit only game species?

Wildlife advocates have the same opportunities as hunters to exert their opinions and viewpoints. Remember, there's no better tactic than emphasizing the economic importance of wildlife protection! The Wildlife Information Center puts it this way in one of its circulars: "The Center believes that the economic benefit of non-killing wildlife recreation far surpasses conventional claims for the economic benefit of hunting and trapping. It believes that when commercial and governmental officials recognize that fact, major changes in government policies regarding wildlife protection can occur. Thus, the Center works to achieve that change." Here are some major ways to help to achieve the necessary change.

Ecotourism

Until recently, wildlife advocates have been slow to grasp the economic importance of ecotourism with a primary emphasis on wildlife. They have been too much the purists, but they're beginning to see the light. Animal rights and wildlife advocates finally are joining bird watchers, whale watchers, the Audubon crowd and others in promoting wildlife and ecotourism.

So, what's ecotourism? No generally accepted definition is available; however, John and Ann Edington provide a good introduction to ecotourism in *Ecology, Recreation and Tourism* (Cambridge University Press). Here are some ecotour characteristics:

🐾 People are taken on supervised trips to spectacular and sometimes remote parts of the world that otherwise they would not be able to visit. Thus, ecotours visit volcanic mountains in Zaire and Rwanda to see the same Mountain Gorillas studied by Dian Fossey, many of the wildlife-rich Galapagos Islands visited by Charles Darwin, vast lengths of the Amazon River explored by Henry Walter Bates, and the astounding plains of East Africa with their teeming wildlife. Small numbers of ecotourists even venture annually to the most spectacular, wildlife-rich shores of the Antarctic on specially designed and constructed expedition ships such as the famous M.S. *Lindblad Explorer*.

🐾 Ecotourists observe and photograph wildlife and other natural history features.

🐾 Educational features of sites and wildlife are stressed. Ecotourists are constantly encouraged to support wildlife protection programs. In areas under major environmental threat, such as Amazon rainforests or the Antarctic, informal discussions are provided throughout tours focusing on the major issues and ways to resolve them.

🐾 Hunting or other harmful activities are not allowed on ecotours. Indeed, ecotours are the nonconsumptive alternative to hunting and trapping.

🐾 Ecotourists are strongly urged not to purchase wildlife products. Good ecotour leaders stress that requirement repeatedly.

🐾 Trained biologists, ecologists and other experts — sometimes world-famous authorities — accompany ecotours and help explain the significance of the sights.

🐾 Every effort is made to avoid damaging sites visited. Any litter dropped by careless participants, including film packaging, facial tissues or other items, is completely removed prior to the departure of the tour.

🐾 Especially sensitive areas with rare ferns, wildflowers or mosses also are carefully avoided, as are wildlife breeding or nesting areas and critical feeding areas.

🐾 Financial donations often are made to selected wildlife and conservation organizations either as additional ecotour fundraising efforts or to underwrite part of the tour.

Ecotourism has become a major worldwide growth industry, yet provides far too little support to wildlife organizations and protection efforts. Although adventure and ecology tours currently comprise only about 10% of the entire two trillion dollar worldwide tourism industry, experts claim that ecotourism is expanding at a 30% annual rate.

Whatever the exact figures, ecotourism means helping keep wildlife alive. The reason is obvious. Ecotourism depends upon living animals thriving in healthy habitats and ecosystems, and people pay money, sometimes dearly, to visit these special places.

Bring money into an area in a regular, systematic manner, allow local residents to share the economic benefits, and people will want to protect the tourist attraction—wildlife. They have a vested interest in the matter, even if for financial gain.

Ecotourism in Kenya, for example, provides a major portion of the nation's income—about $250 million is received annually from 735,000 tourists. That's much more than conventional development could produce for the country. Similarly, according to the *New York Times*, in the State of Amazonas in Brazil, tax incentives formerly given to the cattle ranching industry now are provided to hotels catering to ecotourists.

Money talks, as they say, and wildlife protection can be the winner.

Activism and more formal educational efforts, important as they are, can (and must) follow later. First things first. People seeing, appreciating, and enjoying wildlife are taking the essential first step toward learning to be wildlife advocates. Clearly, ecotourism plays an important role in that process.

Some claim that only prosperous people can afford ecotours; but don't forget that these ecotourists may be key decision-makers for companies whose activities can inflict significant positive or negative impacts upon tropical rainforests, old growth forests of the Pacific Northwest, and countless other important wildlife areas.

Bear Watching

Several forms of bear watching have become a form of ecotourism in North America although details regarding their economic contribution to the overall ecotourism picture are unavailable.

In Alaska, for example, ecotourists can readily observe wild Brown Bears in three locations. The McNeil River State Game Sanctuary on the Alaska peninsula 250 miles southwest of Anchorage gives up to ten ecotourists (per day) outstanding opportunities from early July to mid-August to observe, photograph, and enjoy as many as 106 magnificent Brown Bears as they feed on migrating salmon.

Since Brown Bears are large and potentially dangerous, a strict set of rules are imposed on people at the McNeil Sanctuary. For example, visitors are forbidden to exhibit threatening behavior, while the animals are never allowed to associate food with people. In addition, guides always take ecotourists along the same paths, trails, and viewing areas, and visitors are warned to never stray from them. The result is that the bears now apparently recognize and respect these human areas. Nevertheless, everyone is warned in advance that risk is involved, and they are required to follow the instructions of resident guides exactly if danger develops.

This well-planned Brown Bear viewing site is an excellent example of how people can view large, potentially dangerous wildlife without serious threat to either animal or viewer. More important, Alaska's normally avidly pro-hunting wildlife officials recognize that viewing Brown Bears at the McNeil Sanctuary is one of Alaska's special natural attractions.

On the other hand, at Pine Creek on Admiralty Island about 30 miles south of Juneau, inadequate control of visitors, their behavior, and their bear feeding habits have produced dangerous situations. New restrictions are now in force to reduce bear-people conflicts. We must remember that the bears occupied their feeding sites first; their needs must come first.

In drastic situations, human-animal conflicts may mean closing certain sites to visitors. Wildlife advocates would consider that a small price to pay for assuring the safety and welfare of some of North America's largest and most magnificent carnivores.

Polar Bears are also the focus of ecotourism attention at Churchill, Manitoba, near the shore of the Hudson Bay in Canada. Annually, in October, sixteen to nineteen ecotourists visit Churchill at a time, and from the safety of tundra buggies or special camps observe and photograph Polar Bears frequenting sites close to the town. As more and more people visit Churchill to enjoy Polar Bear watching, regulations have become necessary. Manitoba wildlife authorities are developing guidelines to control activity for the mutual protection of people and bears.

Incidentally, Churchill is also world famous as one of North America's best locations for observing and photographing nesting shorebirds during the summer. Many bird watchers make the foray to Churchill specifically for that purpose, thus adding to the ecotourism economy in this remote town. For a wealth of other natural history information about the Churchill area, read *A Birder's Guide to Churchill* by James A. Lane and Bonnie Chartier.

Black Bear watching also is popular in many of America's national parks. Unfortunately, bears frequently are approached closely and fed by tourists, causing the animals to become pests around campgrounds and along roads in some of the parks. As a result, some animals have become dangerous and have been destroyed by park officials. Wildlife advocates should discourage park visitors from feeding or approaching Black Bears closely.

Bird Watching

Bird watching is the single most popular nonconsumptive wildlife activity in the world. A useful overview of bird watching throughout the Americas (from North America to the Antarctic) is provided in *A Manual for Bird Watching in the Americas* (Universe Books). While statistics on the number of bird watchers vary greatly, depending on the definition of bird watcher, in the United States alone some 61 million people watch wild birds for recreational purposes. Here are some additional facts regarding the importance of bird watching:

◈ Between 300,000 and 1.8 million people in the United States are identified as "committed" to recreational bird watching.

◈ In Pennsylvania, a 1990 statewide recreation survey indicated that 19.4% of the state's population over the age of nine engaged in bird watching, for an average of 123.3 days per year. However, a 1986 wildlife use survey conducted by the Wildlife Information Center indicated that 76% of Pennsylvania's population participated in bird watching.

◈ In Idaho, an estimated 60% of the state's population participates in bird watching.

Many bird watchers are also ecotourists either individually or via taking a commercial birding tour at home and abroad. Indeed, the birds of at least 61 nations are known to attract tourists, with Canada, Great Britain, and Mexico most frequently visited by American bird watchers. These activities have considerable economic value as shown by the following statistics:

◈ In 1981, United States birders spent more than $20 billion on equipment, travel, bird seed and related items.

◈ One recent study suggested that each American birder annually spends an average of $1,852 pursuing the hobby. In 1988, the 43,000 Christmas Bird Count participants alone spent almost $80 million.

Consider some specific significant locations to which bird watchers bring major economic benefits:

◈ In 1988, at Cape May Point, New Jersey bird watchers spent about $6 million.

◈ In 1987, at Point Pelee National Park, Ontario, Canada, the economic value of visiting birders was $6.3 million.

That's economic clout! It also can become political clout, although bird watchers and wildlife advocates have not been able to use that collective power to seek wildlife protection. Sadly, a Yale University study by Stephen R. Kellert indicated that 60% of committed bird watchers approved of hunting, and failed to demonstrate any special ethical concern regarding animal rights or cruel treatment of animals. There's plenty of work for activists to do among these already committed bird lovers.

Most Chambers of Commerce do not recognize the economic benefits that bird watching and other forms of ecotourism can bring to a local economy. Exceptions are Brownsville, Texas, and Winona, Minnesota, both of which produce excellent, colorful promotional literature encouraging ecotourists to their areas. Regretfully, too many business leaders still view wildlife and environmental protection as a business liability.

Business men and women can be taught about the commercial benefits of bird watching or other ecotourism, and the importance of preserving a habitat instead of developing.

Hawk Watching

Within recent years, hawk watching has become one of the major branches of bird watching in Europe, North America, and parts of the Middle East (especially Israel). Once, gunners regularly visited hawk migration lookouts along major raptor flyways such as Bake Oven Knob and Hawk Mountain on the Kittatinny Ridge in eastern Pennsylvania, and Cape May Point, New Jersey, to engage in hawk-shooting activities. They annually slaughtered thousands of migrating raptors at each of these famous locations.

Today, those same lookouts are now major hawk watching sites, a direct result of the intense efforts of raptor protectionists during the 1930s through the 1950s. These days, thousands of hawk watchers, armed with binoculars and cameras instead of shotguns, visit the former death traps to witness spectacular flights of migrating hawks, occasional eagles, and rare falcons.

These hawk watching forays are a classic example of nonconsumptive wildlife activity. What is it worth? Does it have economic value? Indeed, it does! Until recently, little information was available regarding the economic importance of recreational hawk watching. A Penn State University study recently revealed some important economic facts pertaining to Hawk Mountain Sanctuary in eastern Pennsylvania.

&. Visitors pay an average of $5.83 per visitor day on their hawk watching forays.

&. Visitors also indicated, if necessary, they are willing to pay an average of $18.00 per day to engage in hawk watching.

&. More than 46,000 people annually visit Hawk Mountain. The "total resource value" (potential annual economic value) of recreational hawk watching at that single location is more than $577,000 per year.

Curiously, most Chambers of Commerce, usually directly involved in tourism development and promotion, have yet to discover that bird watching in general and wildlife photography provide considerable revenue to local campgrounds, hotels, motels, restaurants, and further income through the sale of other items like gasoline, snacks, and photographic supplies. More money comes in through gift shops operated by wildlife refuges, nature centers, and similar facilities.

Photographic Safaris

Photographic safaris to the spectacular national parks in East and South Africa represent one of the most economically significant forms of ecotourism. Indeed, Kenya derives a major portion of its income from the safari industry. That has resulted directly in the protection of major wildlife areas and huge numbers of animals that otherwise would have been destroyed to make room for other economic activities. Make no mistake about it, in Africa, as anywhere else, money talks. Wildlife must pay its way, or it will be destroyed and replaced with other commercial ventures.

Much the same situation pertains to ecotourism in significant natural areas in Amazonia, Galapagos and the Antarctic — all areas where increasingly large numbers of people are visiting.

Wildlife photography is an equally important and popular activity in the United States, and it provides a particularly acceptable alternative to hunting. Nevertheless, with millions of people now participating in some form of wildlife photography, it is necessary that certain basic rules of behavior be followed to prevent accidental harm to the animals.

🐾 The safety and welfare of a wildlife subject must come before the photographer's desire to take a picture.

🐾 Wildlife should never be put under stress for the sake of a photograph. If a satisfactory photograph can't be taken quickly, the photographer should try later or stop entirely.

🐾 Wildlife breeding and nesting activities should never be disrupted. Only wildlife photography experts, those thoroughly familiar with the biology and ecology of the species, and appropriate photographic techniques, should attempt to photograph nesting birds. Some wild bird species are extremely sensitive to disturbance and will quickly abandon their nests — especially early in the nesting cycle.

🐾 Flocks of migratory birds, such as shorebirds, should not be disturbed when they are feeding or resting at critical stopover points along migration routes. These birds usually are exhausted after completing long stretches of their journey. They need to feed and rest without expending the energy they need to continue their migrations. The same restriction applies to individual birds.

🐾 Predation scenes never should be staged for the benefit of photography.

🐾 Wild animals never should be killed for the benefit of photography.

🐾 Migrating whales should never be approached closely for any purpose, including photography. It is illegal to approach closely endangered cetaceans such as Humpback Whales.

🐾 Endangered and threatened wildlife should be avoided, unless encountered in a natural setting (such as a Bald Eagle or Peregrine Falcon migrating past a hawk watching lookout) which causes no harm or disruption. Endangered and threatened wildlife should not be photographed or disturbed while breeding or nesting; it may be illegal to do so, with stiff fines and penalties imposed for anyone convicted.

Many excellent books about wildlife photography are available. Some of the best include *Nature Photography* by Heather Angel (Fountain Press), *The Complete Book of Nature Photography* by Russ Kinne (Ziff-Davis), *Hunting with the Camera* edited by Allan D. Cruickshank (Harper & Brothers), and *Natural History Photography* edited by E. M. Turner Ettlinger (Academic Press).

Seal Watching

Within recent years, Harp Seal watching on some of Atlantic Canada's ice floes has become the latest important branch of ecotourism, mostly due to the efforts of the International Fund for Animal Welfare. Consider these facts:

🦭 More than 700 people participated in seal watching in Atlantic Canada during one winter. These people each spent between $1,275 and $1,995 to participate in seal watching tours. That's about one million dollars generated by Harp Seal watching!

🦭 Local economies in Nova Scotia and Prince Edward Island derived approximately $600,000 from Harp Seal ecotourists.

🦭 The money that seal watching ecotourists spend in Atlantic Canada is about 20% more than seal killing produced—and the animals are kept alive.

Thus far, Atlantic Canada seal watching ecotourism has not produced jobs for former seal killers (a situation that must change), but it has produced jobs for people working in lodging and restaurant facilities. Some local artists also benefit from the sale of seal-related art items. That's very important. Each time local people receive economic benefits from visitors observing and photographing living seals, the local incentive to keep these animals alive is increased.

Whale Watching

The public has become more aware that recreational whale watching in the Atlantic and Pacific Oceans has become an economically important activity. Here are some facts:

🐋 In California, whale watching produces approximately $2.16 million annually. Primary emphasis is on watching Gray Whales.

🐋 In New England, whale watching produces approximately $4 million annually. Primary emphasis here is on watching Humpback and Finback Whales, although other cetacean species have been observed.

🐋 In Hawaii, whale watching produces approximately $3 million annually. Focus of attention here is on Humpback Whales.

Whale watching obviously is a very popular commercial activity along both coasts of the United States and in Hawaii, and should be encouraged.

However, there is growing concern that some whale watching ships venture too close to whales migrating along the California coast. Some whales have changed their behavior or traditional migration paths. Similarly, in Alaska and Hawaii, conflicts have developed between some whale watching tour operators and government officials, and activists who wish to provide more protection for endangered Humpback Whales. The Alaska Wildlife Alliance is particularly concerned about the affect of tourist ships on whales in Glacier Bay. In 1990 the Alliance filed a lawsuit seeking increased protection for the cetaceans.

The position of the Wildlife Information Center is very clear on these types of problems. Whenever conflicts develop between ecotourism activities and wildlife protection, wildlife protection *always* comes first.

However, one alternative solution to watching whales from boats and ships is to encourage people to watch whales from cliffs and headland sites along the California, Oregon and Washington coasts. Many state parks offer satisfactory whale watching opportunities from land. Of course, before the whale watchers arrive, these sites should be properly regulated to keep the crowd from destroying fragile cliff and headland vegetation, littering the site, or causing other damage. As long as these environmental concerns are addressed, the Wildlife Information Center prefers land-based whale watching, even though observers do not get as close to the cetaceans as they do from ships. California's state and national parks offering whale watching opportunities and, in some instances, interpretive programs, include the following:

- Cabrillo National Monument (on Point Loma)
- Point Reyes National Seashore
- Año Nueve State Reserve
- Fort Ross State Historic Park
- MacKerricher State Beach
- Manchester State Beach
- Mendocino Headlands State Park
- Patrick's Point State Park
- Point Lobos State Reserve
- Salt Point State Park

Wolf Watching

Gray Wolves are among North America's most important, but misunderstood and persecuted, predators. Consider these tragic facts:

- As early as 1683, a bounty was placed on wolves in Pennsylvania. Later, bounties and extermination programs were directed toward wolves in many other parts of the United States and Canada. As a result, wolves no longer inhabit much of their historic range.

- According to information published by the Ontario Trappers Association in *Furbearer Harvests in North America, 1600–1984*, between 1600 and 1984, approximately *1.45 million* wolves were trapped or shot in North America and Russia. As recently as 1953–1954, some 824 wolves were trapped in various Canadian provinces, and an additional 898 in the United States, chiefly Alaska and Minnesota.

- In British Columbia, between 1975 and 1980, the Gray Wolf population was reduced from about 23,000 to 7,000 largely in the name of wildlife management to satisfy the trophy bags of big game hunters.

🐾 Bitter fights still are fought in Alaska where Gray Wolf populations are subjected to persecution. The Alaska Wildlife Alliance is particularly active in protecting Alaska's wild wolves and constantly challenges the policies and programs of the Alaska Department of Fish and Game.

But public attitudes are changing regarding the role played by predators in wildlife communities. That offers hope for wildlife advocates who insist that Gray Wolves should be appreciated rather than persecuted. Limited success is beginning to appear. In a few locations in the United States, and various locations in Canada, Gray Wolves are maintaining or actually are beginning to repopulate their former range. For example, Gray Wolves are slowly reappearing in the Greater Yellowstone ecosystem in the American West and efforts are underway to attempt to reintroduce wolves into Yellowstone National Park (where they were foolishly exterminated earlier in this century).

Wherever these fascinating animals occur, they offer exceptionally important ecotourism opportunities. Watching and listening to wild Gray Wolves is an extraordinary activity when programs have been properly implemented. Here are some important, pioneering examples:

🐾 *Algonquin Provincial Park*. Algonquin Provincial Park, Ontario, a magnificent 7,600-square-mile wildlands area, is one of Canada's largest parks. It is rich in wildlife, including populations of Gray Wolves, which park biologists count by howling themselves and counting the wolves that respond. The Algonquin officials decided to take wolf howling a step further. Between 1963 and 1980, they offered 40 "public wolf howls," and the wild wolves responded 55% of the time. The public's reaction to these innovative events was astonishing. At least 38,477 people attended, an average of 962 people per wolf howl event! Indeed, at times the public wolf howls are too successful: at one 1971 howl, 1,000 disappointed campers had to be turned away.

Algonquin officials correctly point out that hearing wild wolves in this park is a unique experience for almost everyone participating. The amazing popularity of public wolf howls reflects "an extraordinary desire by people for their own, first-hand contact with wolves."

The park's two or three public wolf howls, generally offered during August, are carefully designed, organized, and controlled. Sometimes, as many as 1,000 people (and 250 cars) arrive at the starting point and line up for the opportunity to drive through the dark Algonquin night and hear wild wolves. Dan Strickland, a member of the Algonquin Park staff, describes the effectiveness of successful public wolf howls: "On those occasions when the human howls are answered by a chorus of wolves from somewhere in the surrounding wilderness, the impact on participants is profound and, I think, lasting. No other interpretive event in my experience is so effective in conveying the concept of wildlife and its place in the natural system."

For additional information regarding the park's public wolf howls write to: Park Superintendent, Algonquin Provincial Park, Box 219, Whitney, Ontario, Canada K0J 2M0.

🐾 *Other Canadian Park Wolf Howls.* Public wolf howls similar to those offered in Algonquin Provincial Park also are offered on smaller scales in various other Canadian parks, including Jasper, Prince Albert, and Riding Mountain National Parks, and Sibley Provincial Park in Ontario. Each of these programs has been extremely successful.

🐾 *Adirondack Park, New York.* Although wild Gray Wolves do not currently populate the 6-million-acre Adirondack Park Preserve in upstate New York, serious recommendations have been made to develop a wolf reintroduction program for the park. It is possible that at some future time, public wolf howling programs will be offered in that magnificent area. Wildlife protection activists will want to work closely with organizations such as The Adirondack Council (Box D-2, Elizabethtown, NY 12932) in support of these worthwhile goals.

🐾 *Northern Maine.* Other wilderness areas of the East also are under consideration for Gray Wolf reintroduction projects. According to the November 21, 1990 issue of the *Washington Post*, the extensive wilderness of northern Maine is an area to be investigated and considered for a possible Gray Wolf reintroduction program.

🐾 **Northern Minnesota.** In northern Minnesota, small numbers of wolves maintain viable populations. The International Wolf Center (1900 East Camp St., Ely, MN 55731) offers public wolf howling and other wolf-related educational programs.

🐾 **Isle Royale National Park.** At the time of this writing (December 1990), a small (currently 15), declining population of Gray Wolves exists on Isle Royale National Park in Lake Superior. Whether or not park visitors actually are lucky enough to see these animals is questionable. However, signs of their presence sometimes are visible, which may be enough to satisfy visitors. Unfortunately, the future survival of these animals remains precarious and it is impossible to know whether or not Gray Wolves will survive on Isle Royale in the long-term. Research currently is in progress to attempt to determine the cause of the park's wolf population decline and what, if anything, can be done to reverse the trend.

🐾 **Southern Appalachians.** Another wilderness area under consideration for Gray Wolf reintroduction, according to the *Washington Post*, this time in the Southeast, is the extensive mountain wilderness of Georgia, North Carolina, South Carolina, Tennessee and Virginia.

Watchable Wildlife Programs

Watching and photographing wildlife long has been a popular American activity. However, in 1989, Defenders of Wildlife launched a "Watchable Wildlife" project, the object of which was to greatly expand wildlife viewing opportunities at carefully located and identified national, state and other governmental sites. Details of the Defenders' project were presented in a booklet entitled *Watchable Wildlife: A New Initiative*, written by Sara Vickerman. Wildlife activists may want to secure a copy, study it, then attempt to develop watchable wildlife projects in their area.

According to the *Watchable Wildlife* report, states already participating in these nonconsumptive wildlife projects include:

📖 *Alaska.* Wildlife viewing is a major ecotourism activity for Alaska. Some literature is available, but difficult to secure in most places.

📖 *Colorado.* This state began its Watchable Wildlife program in 1987. Literature and services are available, and emphasis is on encouraging public observation of all types of wildlife.

📖 *Idaho.* The Watchable Wildlife program in Idaho is still small, with the focus on bird watching.

📖 *Montana.* A beginning Watchable Wildlife program is underway in Montana in cooperation with the U.S. Forest Service and the Montana Department of Forestry.

📖 *Oregon.* This state has had an excellent Watchable Wildlife program for more than 10 years. Its highway department uses special road signs to identify appropriate wildlife observation locations. In 1988, an inexpensive ($5.50), 80-page color guide entitled *Oregon Wildlife Viewing Guide* was published which lists and describes 123 locations within the state with wildlife viewing opportunities. The guide also provides information on nearby facilities.

📖 *Wyoming.* This state launched a Watchable Wildlife program in 1986 which includes ecotourism. A particular effort is being made to increase the value of the state's wildlife viewing attractions from an estimated $678 million to $1 billion annually.

Other states also are considering Watchable Wildlife programs. Wildlife advocates should seek opportunities to participate in the development of those programs. These are particularly important opportunities since they allow activists to direct public attention away from hunting and trapping and toward peaceful wildlife uses.

Various federal agencies also are involved in Watchable Wildlife programs. For example, the Bureau of Land Management has produced a color booklet entitled *Watchable Wildlife* which describes some of the best wildlife viewing locations on Bureau property in 13 western states.

Wildlife-Friendly Consumerism

There is a faction in the environmental protection movement called green consumerism. Its basic tenet is that people should only purchase items that have a benign effect upon the environment.

People concerned about wildlife should advocate green consumerism. They should never forget they have a great deal of power—power that the largest companies eagerly attempt to exploit—economic power. Remember, money talks. That's why it's so important that people advocating wildlife protection engage in friendly consumerism. In other words, never buy products that harm wildlife such as:

🐾 All products from endangered species regardless of when or where merchants claim the products were made.

🐾 Fur coats, fur-trimmed coats, fur-lined gloves, or other items regardless if they are made from wild or ranch raised animal pelts.

🐾 Coats, gloves, shoes, handbags, daypacks, or other items made from deer skin.

🐾 Coral jewelry regardless of where in the world the coral is secured.

🐾 Ivory jewelry, regardless of when a merchant claims the ivory was secured.

🐾 Wild birds or other wildlife as pets. Millions of wild birds and other animals annually are robbed from the wild in tropical nations to supply pet dealers in the United States, Europe and other affluent nations. Many of those animals die even before they leave their native land.

🐾 Adopt a wildlife-friendly diet. Avoid buying all meat and poultry products because their production has a serious direct or indirect impact upon many wildlife species and/or their habitats. Some activists also avoid buying fish and all dairy products.

🐾 Do not buy anything from merchants in malls that use traveling animal shows for promotional purposes. (See Chapter 9 for further information.) Be certain to tell merchants in those malls why you boycott their shops. This may stimulate shop owners or managers to ask mall operators not to book and use traveling animal shows.

On the other hand, wildlife-friendly consumers certainly should inform merchants that they purposefully patronize their business because they are a wildlife-friendly merchant. Here's how:

🐾 Print small business cards (on recycled paper if possible) and have a supply ready to hand to anyone in charge of a business whose activities and attitudes you approve.

🐾 Tell merchants that you appreciate their wildlife protection efforts.

🐾 Encourage your family and friends to buy wildlife-friendly products, and ask them to inform cooperative merchants as well.

The sooner retailers become aware that wildlife-friendly policies make good economic sense and will generate increased business, the sooner they will spread the word among other merchants and insist that such policies be put in force.

Money talks! And wildlife benefits.

4

Saving Wildlife Habitat

Wildlife cannot survive without habitat. Thus, to protect wildlife, we must preserve as much habitat as possible.

Hunters long ago recognized this basic need. Wildlife advocates have been slow to learn the lesson. As a result millions of acres of publicly owned wildlife areas are available as killing grounds for hunters.

In comparison, few publicly owned wildlife refuges (where hunting, trapping and fishing are forbidden) exist in the nation. Activists have not produced the funds necessary to buy the appropriate areas. Even the widely respected Nature Conservancy, which *has* preserved some of America's remaining pristine areas, links many of its major fundraising efforts with pro-hunting state and federal wildlife agencies.

Fortunately, habitat preservation for purely wildlife protection is slowly beginning to attract the attention of people opposed to hunting and trapping. In 1990, for example, the Wildlife Information Center established a special fund to buy land for an inviolate wildlife sanctuary. Using fundraising methods ranging from donations to a very successful auction of environmental and celebrity items, the Center raised $7,500 during the project's first year. Much more money is needed, however, and donations are welcome until enough is secured to purchase about 100 acres of woodland and old farmland for use as a wildlife sanctuary.

Once established, the Center's wildlife refuge will permit no hunting, trapping or fishing. While the Center's headquarters will be located on the site, most of the property will be devoted to hands-off wildlife conservation, education and research activities.

Establishing Wildlife Refuges

As more and more land is developed, nothing is more important these days than securing ownership or control of land and establishing wildlife refuges. That's especially true if a 50 or 100-acre tract is adjacent to a much larger forest or other natural area. But even isolated tracts of habitat are useful to many common wildlife species. Here are some basic recommendations for establishing important new wildlife refuges:

Donations. People occasionally donate land to nonprofit organizations (for tax purposes) for use as wildlife refuges, thus creating unexpected but delightful wildlife protection opportunities. Activists should be alert to these possibilities. Among sources of land donations are business, industry, foundations and families or their estates with important properties. Occasionally, a private individual will donate land to a nonprofit organization for wildlife refuge purposes.

Land Swaps. Sometimes, a nonprofit organization receives a real estate donation or bequest of little or no direct value for wildlife protection. It may be possible to swap that property for another that is more useful as a wildlife refuge.

Purchase. Whenever possible, buy an appropriate tract of land outright and thus assure its complete control and use as a wildlife refuge. Although real estate is seriously overpriced in many parts of the nation, properties located farther from urban areas can still be purchased at moderate prices. Check those areas for properties that would make especially attractive wildlife refuges.

🐾 **Grants**. In most cases, when a nonprofit organization decides to purchase land for a wildlife refuge, the fundraising must include efforts to secure major grants from a variety of sources. These sources usually include business, foundations, governmental bodies, industry and individuals. Here are some pertinent considerations:

• Try to identify local businesses that may be sympathetic to the idea of establishing wildlife refuges and are willing to make major donations to the fundraising effort in exchange for income tax relief. In some instances, a donation of land to a nonprofit organization may be part of a court order to settle the prosecution of a company for serious violations of environmental laws.

• Foundation grants can be important sources of wildlife land fund donations. Special efforts should be made to secure such grants whenever possible.

• Many land conservancies receive government aid to buy land for preservation. However, some of these organizations are not wildlife advocates and work closely with government wildlife agencies and hunters. Indeed, in some cases the purpose of protecting land is to maintain locations where public hunting and trapping may continue. The Wildlife Information Center feels that it is unwise to seek government grants for wildlife refuges. Political strings are usually attached and could compromise the objective of wildlife protection organizations.

• More and more private individuals are recognizing the urgent need to preserve land for wildlife. Therefore, make an effort to identify private individuals who are willing to make major donations to land purchase campaigns in exchange for income tax benefits. It is important that these people understand the urgency of this need.

🐾 **Buy Development Rights**. If enough money is not available to purchase land for a wildlife refuge, all may not be doomed. There are less expensive alternatives. One is the purchase of development rights to a desirable tract of land. By acquiring development rights, owners of the property are legally bound to honor the deed restriction. Thus no development ever can take place on the land without the permission of the organization owning development rights. Attorneys experienced in real estate matters can prepare the legal documents necessary for the purchase of development rights to property.

🕮 **Buy Selected Other Rights.** Activists also can buy other types of rights (deed restrictions) including access rights, hunting and trapping rights, logging rights, oil and mineral rights, or the right to any other activities that could threaten a tract of land and degrade or destroy its value as a wildlife refuge. Major conservation organizations such as The Nature Conservancy commonly purchase development rights to significant properties and thus protect them from future development. Wildlife protection activists and organizations will want to go a step further and purchase hunting and trapping rights to assure that these activities will never be allowed on the land.

Arctic National Wildlife Refuge

The Arctic National Wildlife Refuge in northeastern Alaska is one of America's largest and most important wildlife areas. Regretfully, it is under continuing assault by oil companies and misguided federal officials, including those in the White House and Department of the Interior, who seek to allow oil exploration and drilling. The fight to save this magnificent refuge is one of the great wildlife protection efforts of this century. Consider these facts:

🕮 No other area in America compares with the Arctic National Wildlife Refuge's 30,000 square miles (19,049,236 acres) of remote, untouched wilderness.

🕮 The wildlife of the Arctic National Wildlife Refuge has been compared to the vast herds of mammals and other wildlife on the famous Serengeti Plain in East Africa. Vast numbers of rare and beautiful birds and mammals also populate the refuge including

Dall Sheep, Moose, Grizzly Bears, Gray Wolves, Musk Oxen and Polar Bears. At least 142 species of birds live on the refuge.

🐾 North America's largest remaining caribou herds, approximately 200,000 strong, annually migrate over the refuge's coastal plain where oil exploration is proposed. These migrations are among the most spectacular wildlife movements anywhere in the world.

For additional information about this very important wilderness and wildlife area read *Vanishing Arctic/Alaska's National Wildlife Refuge* by T. H. Watkins (Aperture Books).

Antarctica

Anyone given the privilege of visiting the Antarctic comes away with a sense of absolute awe of the nearly pristine and astoundingly rich wildlife and scenic treasures. Antarctica (and the surrounding islands) is the last continent offering environmentalists the ability to preserve nearly untouched nature. For these reasons in 1962 the late celebrated ornithologist and seabird expert Robert Cushman Murphy proposed that Antarctica and key adjacent Antarctic islands be preserved as a World Park — an idea currently promoted by Greenpeace. *Let's Save Antarctica* by James N. Barnes (Greenhouse Publications), *The Greenpeace Book of Antarctica* by John May (Doubleday) and *Beyond the Roaring Forties/New Zealand's Subantarctic Islands* by Conon Fraser (Government Printing Office Publishing, Wellington, New Zealand) provide excellent introductions to the wildlife treasures of the Antarctic and the need to save this magnificent area. The following are some of the actions that activists can take to help save Antarctica:

🐾 Write to the Secretary of State urging the United States to unconditionally support the establishment of Antarctica as a World Park.

🐾 Insist that all government meetings regarding the future of the Antarctica be open to full media and public attendance and even participation.

🐾 Insist that anyone visiting or overwintering in the Antarctic do nothing to harm the area or its unique biota.

🐾 Recruit other wildlife activists to speak out on behalf of the establishment of Antarctica as a World Park. They can do this via media exposure, public education and other means.

🐾 Encourage other animal rights, bird watching, nature study, wildlife and environmental organizations to support full protection for Antarctica.

🐾 Visit the Antarctic on an ecotourism voyage if possible.

For additional information regarding how activists can help save Antarctica, contact the following organizations:

🐾 Greenpeace USA, 1436 U St., NW, Washington, DC 20009.

🐾 Antarctic and Southern Ocean Coalition, 1751 N Street, NW, Washington, DC 20036.

Backyard Wildlife Refuges

There's no place like one's own home turf to begin protecting wildlife. Start with your backyard. Take a look around—especially if you live in a city or populated suburban area. Is it all it could be to attract wildlife? Here are some suggestions:

🐾 Plant trees and shrubs where birds can perch, nest or seek refuge.

🐾 Plant colorful flowers (preferably native species) to attract insects, butterflies and other desirable guests.

🐾 Install bird feeders and bird houses at appropriate locations.

🐾 Preserve natural holes or cavities in dead or dying trees for wildlife's use. Provided they are not a danger to buildings, natural tree cavities are important wildlife homes.

🐾 Use old Christmas trees, or tree and shrub trimmings, to build small brush piles in odd corners of a yard or property to give wildlife protective cover.

🐾 Allow water to slowly drop into a shallow, natural appearing pool. Water is welcomed by almost every backyard wildlife species.

For additional details about developing backyard wildlife

refuges, read *Attracting Backyard Wildlife: A Guide For Nature-Lovers* by Bill Merilees (Voyageur Press) and *American Wildlife and Plants: A Guide to Wildlife Food Habits* by A.C. Martin, H.S. Zim, and A.L. Nelson (Dover). Additional useful books include *The Butterfly Garden* by Mathew Tekulsky (Harvard Common Press), and George H. Harrison's *The Backyard Bird Watcher* (Simon and Schuster). The National Wildlife Federation also has backyard wildlife habitat information available.

Barrier Beaches

Barrier beaches are vital buffer areas protecting the mainland or large islands from the forces of hurricanes and other storms. Regretfully, many barrier beaches along the Atlantic and Gulf Coasts of the United States have been used inappropriately. However, people now are beginning to understand the ecological importance of barrier beaches and are taking the necessary steps to protect those that remain. Here are some outstanding examples:

🐾 The southern six mile portion of Plum Island is protected in its natural condition as a wild and pristine barrier beach.

🐾 Cape Cod National Seashore protects 30 miles of important barrier beaches.

🐾 The Long Island Regional Planning Board recommended that houses and other structures built on Long Island's barrier beaches be gradually removed. The beaches would then be allowed to revert to their natural condition. Wildlife activists applaud this recommendation.

🐾 Fire Island National Seashore protects 32 miles of vital Long Island barrier beaches almost within sight of New York City.

🐾 Island Beach State Park in New Jersey protects a magnificent section of pre-colonial maritime barrier beach.

🐾 Assateague Island National Seashore and adjacent Chincoteague National Wildlife Refuge are 37 miles of barrier beaches supporting famous feral populations of ponies.

🐾 The Nature Conservancy's vitally important Virginia Coast Reserve protects a chain of nine undisturbed barrier beach islands plus four interior islands along the Eastern Shore of Maryland and Virginia.

❧ The unique barrier beaches of Cape Hatteras National Seashore protect 175 miles of vital North Carolina coastline. Some of the beaches extend 30 miles from the mainland into the Atlantic Ocean.

For additional information about barrier beach islands read *Land's Edge/A Natural History of Barrier Beaches from Maine to North Carolina* by Michael L. Hoel (Globe Pequot Press). Do anything you can to save those barrier beach islands not receiving official protection.

Caves

Caves are remarkable wildlife habitats containing some of America's most unusual, and sometimes native, wildlife species. They also are among the most endangered of wildlife habitats. Whenever caves receive public attention and their wildlife is being threatened or destroyed, advocates should act promptly to save these sensitive places. Charles E. Mohr and Thomas L. Poulson provide an excellent introduction to caves, their biota, and their importance in *The Live of the Cave* (McGraw-Hill).

Deserts

Deserts also are endangered habitats. They contain rare and special animal and plant species, including some that are endangered. Activists living near deserts should work hard to save these natural areas. A good introduction to deserts is provided by Jane Werner Watson in *Deserts of the World* (Philomel Books).

Farms As Wildlife Refuges

The possibility of converting countless acres of farmland, old fields, woodlots, wetlands and other areas into an informal, nationwide network of inviolate wildlife refuges provides activists with a spectacular goal. Many state agencies have long attempted to develop cooperative relationships with farmers so that hunters can use farms as hunting areas. Now it is time for wildlife advocates to develop similar relationships with farmers who are opposed to hunting and appreciate keeping wildlife alive on their farmland and, to a reasonable extent, are willing to sustain some crop damage by feeding deer, bear or waterfowl in return for the pleasure of observing them.

Farmland wildlife also offers economic opportunities for farmers. Indeed, innovative farmers having exceptional concentrations of wildlife on their land can convert them into hard cash at little expense. Here are some possibilities:

🐾 Flocks of Canada Geese or Tundra Swans can provide excellent opportunities for bird watchers and photographers. Special blinds can be constructed so photographers can get close-ups of the birds.

🐾 Black Bears or White-tailed Deer that regularly feed in certain farm areas also offer observation opportunities that visitors may be willing to pay for.

🐾 After a visitor program is established on a farm, a small sales shop offering field guides, notecards and like items can augment a farmer's income and increase the farm's popularity.

Properly developed and promoted so that the animals are not disturbed, allowing people to see and photograph without disturbing the wildlife can become another innovative form of farm income. At the same time, wildlife advocates must recognize that they have an obligation to help pay the costs of keeping wildlife alive. It is unrealistic to expect landowners to pay for wildlife protection or crop destruction so that visitors can enjoy free opportunities to see and photograph these wild creatures.

Forest Fragmentation

The impact of forest fragmentation on North American wildlife is increasingly serious. The habitats of a long list of species are threatened by woodland fragmentation. Consider the following facts:

🐾 Human activities that cause fragmentation include highway right-of-way construction, logging, subdivisions and developments, and associated building lots, driveways and access roads.

🐾 Fragmentation causes major ecological change and damage.

🐾 More than 100 forest and woodland migratory, neotropical bird species are threatened by habitat loss in fragmented forests and woodlands. Flycatchers, thrushes, vireos and Wood Warblers are most seriously threatened.

🐾 The same 100 species also are threatened by drastically increased predation by domestic cats and dogs, Blue Jays, Brown-headed Cowbirds, Opossums, and Raccoons. These animals gain access to forest and woodland core areas via highway cuts, access roads, driveways, building lots and logged areas.

🐾 Normal predation rates on migratory birds in large, unfragmented forests are about 2%. Abnormal predation rates on migratory birds in fragmented woodlands range between eighteen and ninety-five percent.

🐾 Different migratory, neotropical birds require different minimums of unfragmented forest to breed successfully. Examples are Great Crested Flycatchers = 3 hectares (1 hectare contains about 2.47 acres), Eastern Wood Pewee = 10 hectares, Wood Thrushes = 20 hectares, Veeries and Ovenbirds = 100 hectares, Black-and-White Warblers = 300 hectares, and Worm-eating Warblers = 1,000 hectares.

🐾 Fragmentation quickly inhibits interior forest species from inhabiting those areas, breeding successfully, and surviving.

🐾 The migratory bird species affected adversely by forest fragmentation in North America are hurt further by the increasing loss of tropical forests in Latin America.

🐾 Unfragmented forests have vital watershed, wildlife and aesthetic values of great public importance which developers and loggers rarely consider.

The Wildlife Information Center strongly recommends that forests and woodlands in North America (especially in New England) be subjected to no further subdivisions, developments or logging. The wildlife and watershed values of these areas require that they be protected and preserved intact in the overall public interest. In addition, in states where very large (500,000 acres or more) unfragmented forests still exist, it is vital that these wildlands remain intact.

Greenways

Wildlife activists are working to save greenways in many communities because:

🐾 Wildlife habitat is preserved, including inter-connecting strips in densely populated areas.

🐾 They provide recreational opportunities including bird watching, hiking, nature photography, canoeing, and similar activities.

🐾 They often contain unique natural features.

🐾 Their aesthetic appearance enhances adjacent property values.

🐾 They have the potential to create jobs related to their maintenance.

🐾 They offer environmental education opportunities in urban and suburban areas.

🐾 Greenways provide excellent sites to stage concerts and outdoor festivals, such as Earth Day.

The U.S. National Park Service (450 Golden Gate Ave., Box 36063, San Francisco, CA 94102) has published an excellent report entitled *Economic Impacts of Protecting Rivers, Trails, and Greenway Corridors* providing extensive documentation useful to those working to establish greenways. Copies are available for the asking. Activists in some communities also are working to incorporate former railroad right-of-ways into greenways. Information on this aspect of greenway programs can be secured from the Rails To Trails Conservancy, 1400 Sixteenth St., NW, Washington, DC 20036.

Land Speculation and Development Impacts on Wildlife

Many organizations are concerned about the impact of land speculation and development upon the environment. Out-of-state land sales companies are active in this and put quick profits at the top of their business priorities. Here are some facts that wildlife advocates should remember when land speculators threaten wildlife habitats:

🐾 Marginal farmland and woodlands typically are purchased and subdivided—often in beautiful rural areas adjacent to public parks and wildlife areas.

🐾 Many rural townships in which land speculators are active have no zoning codes and are wide open for uncontrolled subdivision.

🐾 When communities do not plan for themselves, land speculators do the planning for them. These companies often make major decisions affecting rural communities and environmental quality without public hearings.

🐾 Many land speculators avoid environmental review and regulation when possible.

🐾 Land speculation increases nonresident land ownership.

🐾 Speculators have little interest in the future of the land and its wildlife or even the communities where their subdivisions are located.

🐾 Speculators have knowingly destroyed protected wetlands and other wildlife habitats.

🐾 One land speculation firm's attitude is: "You walk as close to the edge as you can without breaking the law."

🐾 Land speculators are not licensed realtors because they own the land they sell.

🐾 Speculators buy, divide and sell land quickly because of lack of public review.

🐾 Some land speculators advertise rural land in urban newspapers that cater to prosperous urban buyers. Their ads neglect to indicate that large land sales companies are involved.

🐾 Land speculation companies only buy and sell land—they do not develop subdivisions.

🐾 Required roads constructed by speculators generally are of poor quality and only meet minimal standards set by the companies.

Because of these and other problems involved with land speculators and developers, the Wildlife Information Center urges everyone, along with government authorities, to develop state-level regulations or laws that adequately review and control land speculation and development companies. In many areas, such as parts of New England, New York and Pennsylvania, the need for such action is urgent.

National Wildlife Refuges

In September 1989, the U.S. General Accounting Office (GAO) issued a detailed report, *National Wildlife Refuges/Continuing Problems With Incompatible Uses Call for Bold Action*, which documents a distressing quantity of major problems in 60% of 452 national wildlife refuges. In some instances, the problems are so severe that some already endangered species are directly threatened. The report states:

🐾 "National wildlife refuges are frequently not the pristine wildlife sanctuaries implied by their name. While the refuges serve their primary purpose by providing habitat and safe haven for wildlife, virtually all refuges also host many other non-wildlife-related uses. According to refuge managers, managing these secondary uses such as public recreation, mining, and grazing is increasingly diverting management attention from the professional wildlife management functions that refuge staff have been trained to perform. Moreover, despite the requirement that only compatible secondary activities be permitted, refuge managers report that activities they consider harmful to wildlife resources (such as power boating and off-road vehicles) are occurring on nearly 60% of the wildlife refuges."

🐾 "Harmful secondary uses of refuges are occurring for two primary reasons. First, on many refuges FWS has allowed the uses in response to pressure from local public or economic interests. Second, on other refuges FWS has not been able to control the harmful uses because it does not have full ownership of, or control over, refuge lands. Because FWS does not identify the performance potential of each refuge in fulfilling its wildlife enhancement mission, a precise assessment of the overall impact of these harmful secondary uses cannot be made. However, on the basis of refuge manager responses to a GAO questionnaire and GAO's detailed scrutiny of 16 refuges, GAO believes that many of these uses are reducing the ability of refuges to serve their primary purpose."

⊛ Harmful secondary uses allowed on some of the refuges, in descending frequency, are: mining, off-road vehicles, airboats, military air exercises, water-skiing, large power boats, rights-of-way, beach use/swimming, small power boats, grazing, military ground exercises, commercial fishing, hunting dog field trials, camping, waterfowl hunting, haying, picnicking, farming, horseback riding, logging, recreational fishing, non-motorized boats, and small game hunting.

⊛ In national wildlife refuges where managers considered various activities harmful, 97% believed military air exercises should be discontinued, 80% wanted military ground exercises stopped, 77% wanted logging stopped, 68% wanted waterfowl hunting discontinued, 50% wanted small game hunting discontinued, 39% wanted hunting dog field trials discontinued, and 26% wanted recreational fishing discontinued.

⊛ Where harmful activities occurred, external political or community pressure was responsible for waterfowl hunting 80% of the time, recreational trapping 72% of the time, big game hunting 67% of the time, small game hunting 61% of the time, hunting dog field trials 50% of the time, commercial fishing 38% of the time, and military ground exercises 30% of the time.

Major changes in the management of our national wildlife refuges are needed. Activists can contact their Congressmen and the White House, and insist upon returning all national wildlife refuges to purely refuge status. Also, support the Wildlife Refuge Reform Coalition, P.O. Box 18414, Washington, D.C. 20036–8414.

Wetlands Preservation

Wetlands are among the most biologically productive and important habitats in North America (and many other parts of the world). These semi-aquatic lands include bogs, Atlantic coastal and inland marshes, prairie potholes, riparian wetlands of the American Southwest, swamps, tropical rainforests in Hawaii, vernal pools in California, wet meadows and tundra, and similar areas. Here are a few of the many ways they are unique and important:

🐾 Wetlands provide habitat for dozens of species to nest, feed, rest and roost.

🐾 Many endangered species depend upon wetland habitat protection for their survival. Among them are Bald Eagles, Ospreys, Peregrine Falcons, Snail Kites, and Whooping Cranes.

🐾 Wetlands help to maintain and even improve water quality and are especially good water filters.

🐾 They act as gigantic natural sponges that absorb flood waters and help buffer shoreline erosion.

🐾 Many products come from wetlands, including shellfish, timber, blueberries, cranberries, peat moss and wild rice.

🐾 Wetlands offer significant recreational opportunities for hikers, boaters, swimmers, and people seeking to observe some of our nation's most fascinating wildlife species. Regretfully, hunters also intrude upon the wetlands.

🐾 Wetlands are among the most beautiful of all wildlife habitats.

Despite their tremendous ecological importance, wetlands are among the most abused and degraded of all habitats as a result of greed and ignorance. Here are some depressing wetlands loss facts:

🐾 Experts estimate that more than 200 million acres of wetlands existed in the lower 48 states during the 1600s. Currently, less than one-half of those wetlands survive.

🐾 Between the mid-1950s and mid-1970s, approximately 11 million acres of marsh and swamp were destroyed in the United

States. Agricultural drainage was responsible for 87% of those losses.

🐾 The greatest recent loss of wetlands occurred in Arkansas, Florida, Louisiana, Mississippi, Nebraska, North Dakota, South Dakota and Texas.

According to the U.S. Environmental Protection Agency's booklet *America's Wetlands/Our Vital Link Between Land and Water* and the U.S. Fish and Wildlife Service's booklet *Mid-Atlantic Wetlands/A Disappearing Natural Treasure* the following are major causes of wetland degradation and loss:

🐾 Drainage of wetlands.

🐾 Dredging and stream channeling.

🐾 Deposition of fill material.

🐾 Coastal residential development.

🐾 Diking and damming.

🐾 Tilling for crop production.

🐾 Grazing by domestic animals.

🐾 Discharge of pollutants.

🐾 Mining.

🐾 Alteration of hydrology.

Natural threats to wetlands also exist according to the EPA. These include:

🐾 Erosion.

🐾 Subsidence.

🐾 Rising sea levels.

🐾 Droughts.

🐾 Hurricanes and other storms.

🐾 Overgrazing by wildlife.

Can wildlife activists do anything to help save America's priceless wetlands? Yes! Many helpful actions could be taken, and here are some of the most important:

🐾 Develop federal, state and local government policies to protect wetlands.

🐾 Insist that existing wetland protection laws are enforced. That may mean that activists must monitor threats to wetlands as well as actions of federal and state protection agencies.

🐾 Attempt to acquire important wetlands for preservation purposes.

🐾 Work to eliminate government subsidies that encourage wetland drainage and destruction.

🐾 Create state certification programs to train "Wetland Specialists" qualified to identify and delineate the boundaries of wetland areas or ecosystems.

🐾 Insist that entities consider the cumulative impact of ongoing and proposed projects in a locale, not just one isolated project up for approval, before a permit is granted to disturb or alter wetlands.

🐾 Delete wetland replacement (formerly called mitigation) as an acceptable exchange for the destruction of a natural wetland, i.e. agreeing to create an artificial wetland to take its place. Artificial wetlands can never fully replicate natural wetland ecosystems that took thousands of years to develop.

🐾 Work to increase public awareness of the ecological value of wetlands.

🐾 Discourage developers from buying wetlands for subdivision and development purposes.

🐾 Encourage private owners of wetlands to donate those lands to private conservation organizations or public agencies.

🐾 Insist that wetlands be retained as open space.

🐾 Support wetland protection bond issues when they arise.

🐾 Donate money to organizations seeking to buy and protect important wetland areas.

🐾 Secure copies of wetland maps in your area by calling 1–800-USA-MAPS.

🐾 Wetlands in all parts of North America must be protected from further loss.

🐾 Read books such as The Great Cypress Swamps by John V. Dennis (Louisiana State University Press) and other literature pertaining to wetlands.

The Wildlife Information Center suggests that the U.S. Fish and Wildlife and U.S. Postal Services jointly create and sell federal wetlands protection stamps to raise money to buy or protect wetlands without regard for hunting considerations.

Tropical Rainforests

Tropical rainforests are among the most important wildlife habitats in the world. They help to regulate global climate and weather patterns, and are home to a significant portion of the world's animal and plant species. Thus they lay claim to much of our planet's biological diversity. Therefore, from a wildlife protection viewpoint, it is imperative to save the world's remaining tropical rainforests.

Unfortunately, poorly conceived and inappropriate land development projects in Amazonia, for example, have created major problems far beyond the loss of tropical forests. Here are some additional threats to Amazonia's people and rainforests:

🐜 As increasingly large numbers of people move into virgin forests, disease poses serious threats to these very poor people. Malaria is one of the most serious. In 1990, it infected a million or more people in Amazonia.

🐜 Malaria would not have been serious had government officials not encouraged the settlement of tropical forests unsuited for such uses. To combat malaria, the World Bank made a $99 million matching loan to Brazil to spread roughly 3,000 tons of DDT across 2 million square miles of the Amazon basin. DDT, of course, is banned in Canada, the United States and western Europe but is still used widely in many third world nations.

🐜 In many poor nations, 15 species of mosquitoes already are resistant to DDT thus making use of the pesticide useless for malaria control. At least one species of mosquito in Brazil also is resistant to DDT.

🐜 The impact of DDT upon many aquatic bird species and other wildlife is well known. Bald Eagles, Peregrine Falcons, Ospreys, and many other North American aquatic birds suffered major population declines prior to the mid-1970s from DDT contamination of aquatic food chains. Since many North American migratory birds winter in the Amazon basin, they may pick up new and dangerous DDT loads while feeding in their wintering grounds. These birds may again suffer breeding failures and another "Silent Spring" may be in the making—this time generated in Amazonia!

Fortunately, more people worldwide are fighting to save the world's remaining tropical rainforests. The fight to save the Amazon rainforests, among the world's most important, was led by Chico Mendes. The dramatic story of his murder is told vividly by Andrew Revkin in *The Burning Season*. For a nontechnical introduction to saving tropical rainforests read *The Rainforest Book* by Scott Lewis. Here are some important tropical rainforest protection steps, borrowed and adapted from *The Rainforest Book*:

🐾 Avoid buying furniture or other products made from the following rainforest woods:

Apitong	Greenheart	Purpleheart
Banak	Iroko	Ramin
Bocote	Jelutang	Rosewood
Bubinga	Koa	Satinwood
Cocobolo	Lauan	Tea
Cordia	Mahogany	Virola
Ebony	Meranti	Wenge
Goncalo avles	Paduak	Zebrawood

🐾 Educate store owners and product buyers about the need to select items not made from endangered rainforest woods or other materials. Wildlife pets, wild plants, and furniture made from rare tropical rainforest woods should not be sold.

🐾 Do not buy or eat beef, whether produced in deforested tropical areas or elsewhere in the world.

🐾 Buy renewable rainforest nuts and fruits such as Brazil nuts, cashews and avocados. You don't have to buy "gourmet" foods that include these items (although there is nothing wrong in doing so). Just visit your local nut shop or your local farmers' market, supermarket or health food store to buy a variety of exotic tropical fruits.

🐾 If possible, take a vacation and visit a rainforest in Amazonia, Central America, Trinidad, Puerto Rico, the Virgin Islands, Hawaii, or wherever they occur. Ecotours are widely available. There's nothing like visiting a tropical rainforest to fully appreciate these magnificent areas! However, a word of warning. Don't expect to see hordes of wildlife perched openly on every tree. The first impression one has of a rainforest is that little wildlife is present. Even Henry Walter Bates and Alfred Russell Wallace, two of the last century's finest tropical naturalists, were amazed at how little wildlife they encountered upon their first forays into Amazonian rainforests. The reason is because limited numbers of many species are spread over large expanses of forest and dense vegetation, thus making it difficult to see rainforest wildlife. However, the more time one spends in a rainforest, the greater the number of wildlife species one encounters. That's part of the adventure and delight of visiting a rainforest.

Judith Gradwohl and Russell Greenberg describe a number of useful projects and programs in their book *Saving The Tropical Forests* that are helping to save tropical rainforests and their rich diversity of wild species. Some of the most wildlife-friendly include the following:

🐾 **La Amistad Biosphere Reserve, Costa Rica.** This is a mosaic containing more than 500,000 hectares partly in Costa Rica and the rest in Panama. Five Indian reserves and other areas also are included. It is one of Central America's most biologically diverse and important areas.

🐾 **Manu Biosphere Reserve, Peru.** This magnificent area is the world's largest national park covering 1.5 million hectares surrounded by another 300,000 hectares of a sustainable development zone. The area's astonishing biological diversity includes more than 1,000 bird, 13 primate, 110 bat, and more than 15,000 plant species.

🐾 **Amazonia Extractive Reserves, Brazil.** The idea of setting aside extractive reserves for tropical rainforest products such as Brazil nuts, tropical fruits and nuts, rubber, resins, and other plant products was one of the major goals of Chico Mendes. Despite his tragic murder, several extractive reserves now are established, with more planned.

Pacific Northwest Temperate Rainforests

The ancient, old growth, temperate rainforests of the Pacific Northwest are among our nation's most magnificent natural treasures. Included are 1,200-year-old trees, small numbers of Northern Spotted Owls, plus other rare and wonderful species. Indeed, the diversity and richness of wildlife in ancient forests makes the entire region among the most important in North America. Some additional old growth forest facts:

🐾 An unusually large number of bird families occur in the region, including species such as the Northern Spotted Owl, other magnificent birds of prey, the Marbled Murrelet which also may be threatened, Vaux's Swift, and many others.

🐾 Among the 110 mammal species found in these forests, representing 25% of the region's land vertebrates, are Roosevelt Elk, Columbian Black-tailed Deer, Douglas Squirrels, Fishers, and Martens.

🐾 Rare or unique amphibians associated with old growth forests include the Olympic Salamander, Pacific Treefrogs, and tailed frogs.

🐾 Rare or unique vegetation associated with old growth forests includes the Oregon Conk, Oregon White Truffle, and the extremely rare tree fungus known as the "Most Noble" Polyspore (*Oxyporus nobilissimus*) which can weight as much as 300 pounds and live as long as 40 years. Thus far only four or five of these rare fungi have ever been seen. They are the largest fungi found in North America, and may be the largest in the world.

With such biological diversity still intact, it is essential that the remaining 13% of the ancient forests be preserved. Here are some activities that have been attempted to try to save these national treasures:

🐾 Earth First! members and friends organized their 1990 "Redwood Summer" campaign and attracted widespread media coverage for the issue.

🐾 Many traditional wildlife and conservation organizations are actively lobbying Congress and the White House to protect the forests.

🐾 The Wildlife Information Center proposed a carefully planned ecotourism program for the Pacific Northwest's ancient forest region in an effort to provide new jobs for residents currently depending on logging.

The issue of preservation of Pacific Northwest old growth forests still is not resolved, but excellent information is now readily available. In particular, Elliott A. Norse's *Ancient Forests of the Pacific Northwest* contains an impressive treasure of information regarding the entire controversy. Every wildlife activist should read this important book carefully. Then, armed with solid facts, join the battle to save these important national treasures.

Temperate Old Growth Rainforests of South America

It also is important to remember that temperate old growth rainforests occur in South America, especially in Chile. However, until recently, little attention was given to their protection.

Just as the rainforests of the Pacific Northwest are under intense assault, so are temperate rainforests being threatened by the pulp industry in South America. Vast tracts (perhaps one-half million acres) of ancient forest still remain intact in Chile. Here are some basic facts:

🐾 Lumber and pulp companies are actively bidding on the remote southern Chile forests, and their value is increasing. Fortunately, some of the most important stands of alerce are in remote locations.

🐾 Some of these are the same forests that Charles Darwin viewed a century-and-a-half ago during his epic voyage on *HMS Beagle*.

🐾 Among the trees of particular concern to environmentalists is the alerce, a cedar and possible relative of the giant sequoia of northern California. The oldest alerce specimens may be 4,200 years old.

🐾 Araucaria pine and lenga are other important trees native to these ancient forests.

🐾 Collectively, the temperate old growth rainforests of the Pacific Northwest and Chile are the only intact and extensive examples of these special ecosystems. As world ecological and wildlife treasures, their preservation is essential.

Currently, efforts are underway by conservationists in Chile and the United States to purchase several major tracts of Chile's old growth rainforests for preservation. For additional information contact Ancient Forests International, PO Box 1850, Redway, CA 95550.

The Buffalo Commons Project

Currently, a large section of the Great Plains, the shortgrass area, is suffering depopulation as a result of inappropriate agricultural activities, and related economic and social problems. A portion of the Plains is reverting to frontier status, as fewer people live there, and entire communities are depressed or disappearing.

Aware of this unusual situation, Dr. and Mrs. Frank J. Popper of Rutgers University advanced an innovative proposal to deal with declining population trends in the shortgrass prairies. Their idea is to create a "Buffalo Commons" National Park—to restore a major portion of the Plains to its pre-European condition. Here are some of the key elements of this fascinating idea:

🐾 Buffalo Commons National Park would encompass about 139,000 square miles of 10 Great Plains states—an area approximately one and one-half times the size of California—and extend from the 98th meridian westward to the Rocky Mountains. Included would be 109 counties with a declining population of approximately 413,000 people (compared with 6.5 million people living on the entire Great Plains).

🐾 By designating areas unsuited for agriculture as the world's largest national park, and having U.S. government agencies purchase much of the declining or abandoned land, a significant section of the Plains would be converted to its original condition and made into a gigantic wildlife preserve.

🐾 Domestic animals would be removed, presumably in a humane and harmless way.

🐾 A wide range of native wildlife would be reintroduced. Included would be 75,000 bison, 150,000 deer, 40,000 elk, and 40,000 antelope, plus a wide range of other native wildlife.

🐾 Birds of prey found in the area would be an important part of the park's wildlife treasures.

🐾 Like the magnificent six million acre Adirondack Park in up-state New York, the proposed Buffalo Commons National Park would be composed of a combination of pubic lands intermixed with private holdings.

🐾 The park's land would be secured gradually as the region continues to become depopulated.

🐾 Ecotourism, such as exists in major East African national parks, would be among the benefits resulting from the wildlife reintroductions. The ecotourism would focus on wildlife photography.

Thus far, people hearing about the proposed Buffalo Commons project are either very enthusiastic or hate the idea. In fact, in many parts of the Plains people are so opposed to the idea that bodyguards are present when the Poppers make presentations in various communities. Nevertheless, the idea and data supporting it have great merit and deserve implementation.

Various articles have been published about the Buffalo Commons project including Dayton Duncan's "Westward, NO" (*Boston Globe Magazine*, June 10, 1990), Ruth Eckdish Knack's "The Poppers Strike a Nerve" (*Planning*, May 1990 issue. PP. 20–22), Anne Matthews' "The Poppers and the Plains" (*New York Times Magazine*, June 24, 1990), "The Great Plains: From Dust to Dust" by Deborah Epstein Popper and Frank J. Popper (*Planning* , December 1987 issue. PP. 572–577), and "Saving the Plains: The Bison Gambit" by Frank J. Popper and Deborah Epstein Popper (*Washington Post*, August 6, 1989).

Additional information regarding the Buffalo Commons project can be secured from Dr. Frank J. Popper, Department of Urban Studies and Community Health, Lucy Stone Hall, Rutgers University, New Brunswick, NJ 08903.

Sites of Special Importance

Throughout the United States (and elsewhere in the world) sites of special importance in the history of the conservation movement exist, and are viewed as special because of their unique wildlife or environmental features. Most of these have been identified and protected by some governmental agency, nonprofit organization or private interest. Occasionally, however, a site of special importance is threatened by development or some other inappropriate use or impact. In those cases, it is important that wildlife activists try to lend support to help assure protection of the site. Some appropriate types of support are:

🐾 A formal letter written on an organization's letterhead supporting preservation of the site.

🐾 Donations of money, or services as needed, to the lead organization working to protect the site.

🐾 Making statements to media in support of preservation of the site.

🐾 Providing special technical assistance, when requested, to the lead organization working to protect and preserve the site.

🐾 Assisting in other ways as may be deemed helpful including close cooperation with organizations with similar concerns.

Walden Pond in Concord, Massachusetts, forever preserved for following generations of readers and advocates of nature preservation in *Walden* by Henry David Thoreau, is an outstanding example of a site of special importance that was threatened by development and other inappropriate uses. Leading the fight to protect and preserve Walden Pond was Mary Sherwood representing Walden Forever Wild. In 1990, she was aided by rock singer Don Henley, who served as co-chairman of the Walden Woods Project, which worked with the Trust for Public Lands and purchased a key 25-acre parcel of Walden Woods for $3.55 million where a 139-unit housing development had been planned. Efforts also are underway to save certain other key sections of land around Walden Pond.

5

Reforming Wildlife Policy

P rotecting wildlife involves more than nailing "No Hunting" signs to trees on wildlife refuges, banning leghold traps, or buying wildlife habitat for use as a refuge. Although these are important activities, we also need to stimulate new public attitudes regarding the relationship of people with wildlife, and reforming wildlife laws, and policies.

Progress is being made. Changes are slowly taking place in state wildlife agencies, within the U.S. Fish and Wildlife Service, and among wildlife professionals. Consider these examples:

🐦 Birds of prey are now federally protected after decades of intense public education and legislative efforts by raptor conservationists.

🐦 The federal Endangered Species Act provides critical protection to seriously threatened or endangered wildlife thus preventing many of these species from becoming extinct.

🐾 Treaties such as CITES provide further international protection to endangered and other wildlife species.

🐾 Various laws provide some degree of protection to wild animal and plant species.

🐾 An increasing number of articles discussing animal rights, wildlife protection, and conservation biology are appearing in professional wildlife journals, newsletters, and periodicals, including *Ornithological Newsletter, Wildlife Review* and *Wildlife Society Bulletin.* Although some are openly hostile toward opponents of hunting and trapping, others are moderate and open-minded. Thus the wildlife profession is beginning to examine protection points of view that were previously ignored. That's the first step toward accepting wildlife protection as a basic policy.

However, it's important to understand that wildlife laws don't just happen by themselves. They can be the result of decades of legislative effort by concerned people who might be advocates of total wildlife protection. Nevertheless, the message is clear. Changing wildlife policy requires determination, lots of hard work, and a range of skills beyond simply communing with nature. In fact, major land preservation organizations such as The Nature Conservancy have a policy not to mix business (the mechanics of making land preservation deals) with appreciation of nature. Their biologists conduct field surveys to evaluate the ecological importance of various properties being considered for preservation, then lawyers and MBAs take over to make the deals. Similarly, when attempting to change wildlife policy, one size does not fit all!

Thus, to be effective at wildlife protection in today's complex political climate, the skills of many people must be used when dealing with public officials. Generally, those involved with legislation are city or county officials, state representatives, or members of Congress, while state wildlife agency or U.S. Fish and Wildlife Service officials deal with other matters. Depending upon the nature of an effort, lobbyists, lawyers, business experts, public relations professionals and other experts may be necessary. Following are some typical, basic means of achieving increased wildlife protection.

Informal Recommendations

One of the most important, but least expensive ways to promote a change in wildlife policy is to make a recommendation to legislators or agency representatives. The adoption of a new law or regulation might be the target, and in either case, a specific aspect of wildlife policy generally is addressed. It is unrealistic to expect to write a single law or regulation that would achieve sweeping policy changes. Therefore, activists seeking new laws or regulations must carefully define what they are trying to accomplish and focus on specific issues (such as banning the use of leghold traps) pertaining to specific areas of wildlife law, regulation or policy.

Legislative Action

Seeking a legislative change in wildlife policy, either at the federal or state level, is one of the most common opportunities available to wildlife advocates. And, it sometimes takes years or even decades of continuing work to secure an appropriate new law. However, once enacted and properly enforced, new laws providing added wildlife protection are worthy. Some steps necessary in securing new legislation are:

&. Identify a specific wildlife issue and determine what new legislation is necessary.

&. Make a list of specific points to be included when the proposed legislation is written.

&. Secure the cooperation of a legislator, or better still a bipartisan group of legislators, to sponsor and introduce the bill.

&. Secure the active cooperation of as many people and organizations as possible to urge legislators to support the bill.

&. Present testimony at any public hearings held regarding the bill. Many bills never receive public hearings, but it is not unusual for complex or controversial bills to receive at least one formal public hearing so that organizations and government agencies can state their concerns. Unfortunately, some bills also die in committee after public hearings are held.

🐾 If necessary, secure professional lobbyists to help push for passage of the bill.

🐾 Thank cooperative legislators for their help, whether the effort succeeds or not.

Endangered Species Act

The worldwide number of endangered wild animal and plant species is growing at an appalling rate. The Endangered Species Act figures as one of the most important United States wildlife protection laws. Without the Endangered Species Act, there would be many more extinct wild animal and plant species. Any activities that could weaken or destroy the Act are of major concern to conservationists. Regretfully, the Endangered Species Act faces many threats:

🐾 Most endangered species are not yet officially listed by the United States, and the rate of progress is unacceptably slow. Activists should insist upon a much faster listing rate.

🐾 Both commercial interests and government agencies increasingly are finding the Endangered Species Act an obstacle to their plans. They do try to overcome it in one way or another. Let us hope they fail in every case! The purpose of the Endangered Species Act is to protect endangered species and even to attempt to restore those species to reasonably adequate population levels so they can be de-listed.

🐾 Some powerful business interests, and certain politicians, seek to weaken or even eliminate the Endangered Species Act. Timber and oil interests are especially opposed to limitations imposed upon their activities by the Act.

🐾 The Secretaries of the Interior in several recent administrations did not adequately enforce the Endangered Species Act.

🐾 The U.S. Fish and Wildlife Service is not fully meeting its duties in administering the Endangered Species Act.

These problems are serious. They should be of major concern to every wildlife advocate who can take action to help assure enforcement of the Endangered Species Act.

&. Write, telephone or visit your Congressman and express unconditional support for a strong Endangered Species Act.

&. Express similar concerns to the White House and the Secretary of the Interior.

&. Help to educate the public about the Endangered Species Act by writing letters-to-the-editor of your local newspaper.

&. Call radio call-in talk shows on occasion and discuss the importance of the Endangered Species Act.

&. Work to reduce and eliminate those threats to wildlife that cause a species to become endangered.

The Wildlife Information Center is doing all it can to make absolutely sure the Act prevails and continues to provide strong protection for the endangered animals and plants whose *species survival* depends upon this vital wildlife protection law.

Legal Action

One of the most expensive, but unrealistic ideas of advocates seeking changes in wildlife policy is that legal action should be the primary technique used to secure reforms in wildlife laws. Make no mistake about it, legal action sometimes is successful, but professionals know that lawsuits usually are the last resort. Going into court usually signals that all other methods to alter a policy (or enforcing an existing law or regulation) have failed. Legal action requires complex and expensive preparation with appeal to higher courts often a likelihood.

Regretfully, wildlife advocates have often sued to reform federal or state wildlife policies and lost. Sometimes they did not prepare their cases adequately. Failure usually means they lacked professionally prepared ecological data to support the legal action rather than a poor performance by their lawyers. In some instances, they failed to appeal lower court decisions.

It is wise to use legal action only if adequate information is available and a suit is the only remaining option. If legal action is your last inevitable resort, here is a list of legal groups that may be able to help:

🐾 Animal Legal Defense Fund, 1363 Lincoln Ave., Suite 7, San Rafael, CA, 94901, (415) 459-0885. Additional chapters are located in parts of the United States.

🐾 Rutgers Animal Rights Law Clinic, School of Law - Rutgers (Newark Campus), (201) 648-5989.

🐾 Sierra Club Legal Defense Fund, Inc., 2044 Fillmore St., San Francisco, CA 94115, (415) 567-6100.

Regulatory Action

It also is possible to secure changes in federal and state wildlife policies by altering regulations. These regulatory actions can take various forms. The following are the most common and important:

🐾 *Formal Petitions.* At the federal level, and usually regarding the U.S. Fish and Wildlife Service but occasionally regarding other agencies such as the Bureau of Land Management, Environmental Protection Agency and National Park Service, the use of formal petitions sometimes can produce desirable changes in the Code of Federal Regulations (CFR). In deciding to petition activists must prepare accurate, well-documented research that explains the issue, why a change is desirable, and that contains solid scientific data to support the proposed rule change. The formal petition and cover letter is then mailed (or even hand-delivered) to the appropriate official. When dealing with government agencies such as the Bureau of Land Management (BLM), National Park Service, or U.S. Fish and Wildlife Service, formal petitions normally are sent to the Secretary of the Interior or perhaps the Director of the BLM, National Park Service, or U.S. Fish and Wildlife Service.

🐾 *Public Hearings.* At some stage in the complicated process of changing regulations to increase protection for wildlife, public hearings may be announced and held by the agency proposing the regulatory change. It is important that advocates participate by presenting carefully prepared testimony—even if only to get alternative viewpoints on the official record and deny government officials any opportunity to state they did not know about alternative positions and options.

Often it is necessary to notify the agency before the public hearing that you wish to be added to the speaker roster. Sometimes written notice is required, at other times telephone calls are acceptable. Whichever form of notification is required, it should be done promptly—especially if the matter is of great concern.

Actual testimony should be carefully researched and fully written out, with extra copies available for each member of the agency holding the hearing. Find out the number of copies of testimony they require. Save copies for your own files, and have another handful for media covering the hearing. News releases containing highlights of your testimony also can be distributed at the hearing.

&. *Freedom of Information Act.* Sometimes federal agencies are uncooperative in providing information requested. In those instances, the Freedom of Information Act's provisions may require the uncooperative agency to provide the necessary information. Freedom of Information Act requests should be specific, and directed to the appropriate agency or department's Freedom of Information Act officer. It may be necessary to pay photocopy charges if large quantities of documents are requested.

Voting For Wildlife Protection

The number of people who advocate wildlife protection yet never vote in general elections is astonishing and depressing. In the final analysis, elected public officials at all levels of government are the ones who approve or reject laws that determine the fate of wildlife. Not voting for sympathetic candidates almost assures that legislation favoring hunting and trapping will continue at the state and federal levels. The obvious solution is to become an informed and regular voter—what some politicians call "supervoters."

Although a single vote rarely decides an election, if large numbers of people vote for acceptable candidates, it won't be long before wildlife policies begin to change and reflect more acceptable degrees of wildlife protection. This is the most fundamental part of the American system—and one that hunters and trappers long ago learned to use to their benefit. It's high time serious wildlife advocates use the same technique!

Voting in general elections also offers opportunities to accept or reject resolutions, referendums and bond issues for specific wildlife or environmental programs. Voting on those matters is important. Indeed, the failure of large numbers of activists to vote can cause the defeat of key wildlife protection efforts. That was vividly demonstrated during many November 1990 state elections when key environmental issues were put before the voters. According to *Common Ground*, a newsletter published by The Conservation Fund in Virginia, the following are some of the confusing and contradictory results of those elections.

🐾 *Arizona.* Sixty-four percent of voters opted to dedicate $20 million annually in lottery proceeds to various conservation uses.

🐾 *California.* Voters seriously defeated several important environmental options.

🐾 *Florida.* Voters approved by 60 percent $20 million in land purchase bonds. Another $100 million bond act for land purchase was approved by 73 percent several weeks earlier in Hillsborough County. Collectively, Florida voters approved the sum of $565 million for conservation purchases during the next year.

🐾 *Maine.* Voters rejected two measures providing for $5 million in parks improvements (47 percent to 53 percent) and $19 million in land purchases (41 percent to 59 percent). Confusing ballot language contributed to these defeats.

🐾 *Minnesota.* The voters gave 80 percent approval for a constitutional amendment to dedicate 40 percent of state lottery proceeds to Minnesota's Natural Resources Trust.

🐾 *Missouri.* Voters defeated by 3 to 1 a Natural Streams Act.

🐾 *New Mexico.* A 54 percent voter majority rejected a $225,000 bond act to buy endangered species habitat.

🐾 *New York.* In one of the most serious defeats for wildlife, 51 percent of voters rejected a $1.975 billion conservation bond measure that would have purchased and preserved significant wilderness areas in the Adirondack Park. Residents within the park area voted as much as 10 to 1 against the measure.

🐾 **Nevada.** Voters indicated by a 66 percent approval a $47.2 million bond issue for parks, wildlife and land protection.

🐾 **Oregon.** Voters rejected several environmental options including 59 percent who chose not to close down the Trojan Nuclear Plant.

🐾 **South Dakota.** 53 percent of voters approved a measure to regulate large, solid-waste landfills, but a similar percentage of voters wanted no controls put on surface mining in the Black Hills.

🐾 **Washington.** Voters rejected by 3-to-1 a "slow-growth" statewide land use measure. While San Juan County adopted a real estate transfer tax to fund land purchases, six rapidly growing counties around Puget Sound rejected the same option.

6

Wildlife Management Techniques

W hen a vivid bolt of blue flits across a rural road and an Eastern Bluebird lands on a bluebird box atop a fence post along the edge of an old meadow, the value of wildlife management has been witnessed.

Indeed, without such "bluebird trails" extending along thousands of miles of country roads in the United States and Canada, bluebird populations would be severely reduced, if not endangered. Nest box projects also are established for Tree Swallows, American Kestrels, Barn Owls, Screech Owls and other species.

With so many species to deal with and so much growing interest in wildlife management, much information has been published pertaining to management techniques. Much of this focuses on ways to increase populations of so-called game species for the benefit of hunters, but other techniques are designed to aid non-game wildlife, and some specific groups of species such as raptors. The most commonly used summaries of wildlife management techniques are listed below.

⚘ *Wildlife Management Techniques Manual* edited by Sanford D. Schemnitz (The Wildlife Society) summarizes conventional thinking of game managers. Wildlife advocates strongly disagree with the reasons for this approach and many of the techniques.

⚘ A summary of management techniques for parks and wilderness areas is provided in *Ecosystem Management for Parks and Wilderness* by James K. Agee and Darryll R. Johnson.

⚘ Raptor management is summarized by Beth A. Giron Pendleton and associates in *Raptor Management Techniques Manual*.

In general terms, wildlife management techniques are either active or passive. Most techniques are active, but a few passive methods also can be effective in appropriate instances.

Active Wildlife Management

Installing bird feeding stations, placing nesting boxes, or planting trees, shrubs and other vegetation to improve habitat are examples of active wildlife management. Too many conservationists believe that wildlife management is used only to produce unnaturally high populations of game animals for the benefit of hunters and trappers. Nothing could be farther from the truth!

Conservation biologists who deal mostly with non-game species frequently select from a wide range of techniques to help protect specific wildlife species. So, too, do many ordinary people. Here are some relatively easy-to-use management methods of great benefit to non-game wildlife:

⚘ ***Bat Houses.*** Installation of bat roosting houses can significantly aid these badly misunderstood but valuable, insect-eating mammals.

⚘ ***Beavers.*** Beavers are magnificent animals that play important roles in creating wetlands and providing habitat for numerous species. Occasionally, they build dams in undesirable locations. Humane methods of dealing with these problems include live-trapping and relocating the animals, and the use of "Beaver

Bafflers" which prevent them from using culverts under roads. For details, request a copy of the "Beaver Problems and Solutions" fact sheet from The Beaver Defenders, Unexpected Wildlife Refuge, Inc., P. O. Box 765, Newfield, N.J. 08344. "Beaver Baffler" information also is available (include a SAGE) from Friends of Beaversprite, Box 591, Little Falls, N.Y. 13365. Canadians can secure information regarding the "Thurber Beaver Stop" from Beaver Stop Consulting, Inc., 3219 Coleman Road, NW, Calgary, Alberta T2L 1G6.

🐾 *Birdhouses.* Birdhouses can provide valuable nesting sites for many birds such as Wood Ducks, Bluebirds, House Wrens, Tree Swallows, Purple Martins, American Kestrels, Barn Owls and Screech Owls. A good source of information featuring birdhouse construction is *Classic Architectural Birdhouses and Feeders* by Malcolm Wells. Activists wanting to help bluebirds should read *The Bluebird* by Lawrence Zeleny.

🐾 *Bird Feeders.* Installation of bird feeders provides visiting birds a regular food source. Most bird watchers use both seed and suet feeders, but some advocates recommend substituting suet with peanut butter. Continue supplying feeders throughout the winter so that birds dependent upon them will not suddenly be faced with no food supply. *A Complete Guide to Bird Feeding* by John V. Dennis and *The Expert's Guide to Backyard Birdfeeding* by Bill Adler, Jr. and Heidi Hughes contain information regarding the most effective ways to operate bird feeders.

🐾 *Planting Vegetation.* In most backyards, it is desirable to plant additional native vegetation to provide food, shelter and nesting sites for birds. Selection of trees, shrubs and wildflowers depends on where you live. *American Wildlife and Plants: A Guide to Wildlife Food Habits* by A.C. Martin, H.S. Zim, and A.L. Nelson is a good source of information regarding the selection of vegetation for backyard planting.

🐾 *Butterfly Gardens.* Establishment of butterfly gardens is gradually becoming popular. Planting selected species of native wildflowers is most important in the establishment of butterfly gardens. Additional details are provided by Mathew Tekulsky in *The Butterfly Garden.*

🐾 ***Wildlife Fertility Control.*** Among the techniques at the leading edge of wildlife management is the use of fertility control methods on selected wildlife populations. Recently, for example, an experimental vaccine for White-tailed Deer proved to be effective in research trials. In due time it may help to regulate deer populations in ecological islands such as isolated parks surrounded by housing and other development. Fertility control methods are used in other parts of the world, as in South African national parks to regulate African Lion numbers. It must be understood, however, that fertility control methods are very new and not designed for large populations living in extensive wildland areas. Nevertheless, they may help reduce the need for deer hunting in restricted urban and suburban areas.

Passive Wildlife Management

As its name implies, passive wildlife management involves a hands-off policy where nature takes its course. Allowing an old field to grow back into woodland is an example of passive management. As wildflowers that once lived in the old field are replaced by shrubs or trees, and they in turn are replaced by other tree species—a process known as ecological plant succession—different species of birds and other wildlife begin to appear as conditions become more favorable to their needs.

Black Bear Encounters

The Black Bear is the largest carnivore widely distributed throughout most of the United States. In some sections of the country, such as the northeast, housing developments now occupy former wildland areas bringing more city-oriented people into contact with Black Bears. In most instances, the bears will attempt to avoid people. However, bears can become habituated when fed human food. Habituated bears can become problems—or even dangerous. The following are important facts to consider regarding bear-human relations:

🐾 From 1900 through 1980, only 500 people have been injured by Black Bears across all of North America.

🐾 More than 90% of Black Bear injuries were minor, but 35 injuries were major including 23 human deaths. Records of 20 fatal cases show that 50% involved people age 18 or younger, and 5 were younger than 10 years.

🐾 Limited evidence suggests that young people may be more susceptible to fatal Black Bear attacks than older people. The reason for this is unknown.

Based upon the best available information the following precautions **may** help avoid close Black Bear encounters when traveling on foot in bear country.

🐾 NEVER throw away food scraps, including apple cores or banana peels, or allow human food to remain in the open.

🐾 NEVER establish bear feeding stations near buildings! This only invites bears to become habituated to food handouts, concentrate around dwellings, and perhaps invite problems, house damage, and injury to people.

🐾 Be alert when walking in bear country.

🐾 NEVER attempt to feed a bear if one appears at close range!

🐾 Do not throw stones or other objects at a bear!

If you see a Black Bear at a distance of 300 feet or more, try to maintain that distance. Do not panic. Attempt to use some or all of the following options:

🐾 Try to detour around the bear, and maintain a good distance from it.

🐾 From a safe distance, wait until the animal leaves the area and enjoy your good fortune in seeing it. However, keep in mind that the animal may have bedded down close to the trail and therefore is still near you.

🐾 If the animal seems to have left the area, return making plenty of loud noise and remaining fully alert. Loud noise may cause the bear to move off.

🐾 If, for any reason, you still believe the bear is in the vicinity and poses a threat cancel your visit and leave the area. Although it is rarely necessary to do this, ignore foolish ridicule from other people.

If you unexpectedly encounter a Black Bear at a close distance (less than 300 feet), particular care should be taken because each bear may react differently or according to its feelings at that moment. However, bear experts recommend the following actions:

🐾 Do NOT run; the bear will likely chase you. It can run faster than you can! If the bear rears onto its hind legs, it is trying to investigate you and decide what to do.

🐾 Immediately, WITHOUT SUDDEN MOTION, look for a tree to climb at least 12 feet above the ground. While retreating to the tree, drop something interesting from your pack to briefly distract the bear. If you climb the tree, remain there at least 30 minutes after the bear has left. Bears are patient and cagey animals.

🐾 If no suitable tree is available, and the bear seems uninterested and has not acted aggressively, slowly back away while talking softly and waving your arms. DO NOT STARE AT THE ANIMAL.

🐾 If actually under attack, PLAY DEAD. Drop to the ground, roll up in a ball, and cover the back of your neck with your hands. DO NOT YELL OR STRUGGLE, even if the bear sniffs or paws you.

Lawn Care Chemicals and Pesticides

As more and more people become aware of the survival needs of wildlife, especially in urban and suburban areas, much greater emphasis is being placed on the need to be very careful and restrictive in the use of lawn chemicals and pesticides. Many people now are very concerned about the environmental and health impacts of the application of lawn care chemicals which contain pesticides, herbicides, insecticides and other compounds. Before using these toxic compounds here are some important points to remember, based in part upon information provided by New York State Attorney General Robert Abrams in his 1987 booklet *Lawn Care Pesticides: A Guide for Action* (Office of the Attorney General of New

York State, Department of Law, Environmental Protection Bureau, Albany, New York):

🐾 Lawn care chemicals are suspected of having grave health effects on pregnant women, elderly people, small children, chemically sensitive people, asthma and allergy sufferers, pets and wildlife. Take strong safety precautions!

🐾 Be aware that insecticides, herbicides and pesticides used by lawn care companies, and those which are contained in over-the-counter products, are very toxic and dangerous. One example is the infamous Agent Orange, an herbicide still used today that is strongly suspected of having neurologically crippled many Vietnam veterans.

🐾 Consumers cannot assume that chemicals registered with the Federal Insecticide, Fungicide and Rodenticide Act (FIFRA) are safe and will not pose a danger. Many of the chemicals are being re-tested for safety by new, more sophisticated methods.

🐾 Do not assume "inert" ingredients to be safe! Many lawn care products list chemicals which are not "active" (meaning killing) ingredients as "inert" ingredients. "Inert" chemicals carry or dissolve the "active" chemicals. They do not meet the same test requirements as "active" chemicals yet they can be known toxins such as asbestos and benzene.

🐾 As a consumer, demand a complete list of chemicals to be sprayed, along with precautions to take to protect yourself before the date of applications.

🐾 Be aware of companies that do not send "certified" chemical applicators and whose employees are not wearing protective gear such as gloves and respirator. Applicators who are not properly trained pose a danger to the public. They may also provide inaccurate answers to consumer questions.

🐾 The most dangerous problem with lawn chemical application is inevitable chemical migration. They will drift in wind and run-off in rain. Never apply the chemicals on a windy day, on steeply sloping areas, or near streams and ponds.

🐾 Don't let ads lull you into thinking that lawn care chemicals are safe. Consumers must weigh the benefits of a greener lawn against uncertain long-term health problems. Remember, the spraying of potentially hazardous lawn care chemicals is an intentional act of chemical exposure to yourself, your family, pets and wildlife.

In view of the potential dangers imposed by the use of lawn care chemicals and pesticides, wildlife advocates are encouraged to use much less dangerous techniques on their lawns and home gardens. Consider using the much more preferable organic lawn care and gardening methods for which plenty of excellent information now is available in libraries, from many county agricultural agents, and published by firms such as Rodale Press, 33 E. Minor St., Emmaus, PA 18049.

Reducing Wildlife Roadkills

Anyone who drives America's highways can't help but notice the appalling number of dead animals littering our roads — tragic reminders of wildlife-vehicle collisions. Mostly, people give up in despair and assume nothing can prevent this unfortunate highway slaughter. In fact, efforts are underway to reduce the highway roadkill problem and progress is being made in some instances.

Consider deer-vehicle collisions which are among the most serious and expensive types of wildlife roadkills. In 1989, in Pennsylvania alone more than 40,000 deer were reported killed along the state's highways; doubtless many more went unreported. Many other states also suffer very high numbers of deer-vehicle collisions. Here are some suggestions for reducing deer-vehicle collisions:

&. *Drive Defensively.* Drive defensively, and within posted speed limits. Slow down if you see deer anywhere along the sides of the highway on which you are driving.

&. *Observe Deer Crossing Signs.* Note deer crossing warning signs. Slow down when approaching, and passing through those areas.

&. *Note Deer Crossing Areas.* On highways along which you

drive frequently, make a mental note of where you see deer. Be particularly careful when driving past those areas.

🦌 **Be Especially Alert At Dawn and Dusk.** When driving along new highways, or when passing through areas with old fields adjacent to woodlots or woodland, remain particularly alert just prior to and after dawn and dusk and at night.

🦌 **Watch For Multiple Deer Crossings.** Deer usually do not travel alone, so remain alert for more than one animal crossing a highway ahead of you. Also keep in mind that a deer crossing ahead of you may double back, or move into the path of another approaching vehicle. Do not swerve into the path of an oncoming vehicle to avoid hitting a deer! Hitting a deer usually is less serious than causing a head-on collision with another vehicle.

🦌 **October to December Are Dangerous Months.** Deer-vehicle collisions can occur during any month, but October through December are the peak months for these accidents to occur. Deer are then in rutting season, and hunters roaming fields and woodlands are disturbing natural behavior and movement patterns of the animals.

🦌 **Ultra-sound Whistles Need More Study.** Ultra-sound whistles that mount on vehicle bumpers, are said to prevent deer-vehicle collisions but they may not be effective. However, they are relatively inexpensive so until conclusive studies demonstrate their ineffectiveness, motorists may wish to continue using them.

🦌 **Swareflex Roadside Reflectors.** The State of Washington decided to do something that would prevent deer-vehicle collisions, and began experimental use of Swareflex roadside reflectors. Test results from these devices showed a 90% reduction in deer-vehicle collisions in that state in carefully controlled field trials. Today, some 35 states and Canadian provinces are at least experimenting with these Austrian-developed reflectors. A few states, including Minnesota and Washington, are beginning to use them routinely at appropriate locations along their highways.

Unfortunately, highway departments and state wildlife agencies in many states are uncooperative regarding the use of Swareflex reflectors. Some states even attempt to prevent their use. That's tragic. When Swareflex reflectors are installed correctly and placed

at appropriate locations, they can help reduce deer-vehicle collisions, prevent death and injury to people and wildlife, and prevent
expensive damage to vehicles. For additional information regarding the use of Swareflex reflectors to help reduce deer-vehicle collisions, call the Strieter Corporation, Inc., (309) 794–9800.

Collisions of deer with vehicles, of course, are not America's
only serious roadkill problems. Many smaller animals such as
opossums, skunks, squirrels, raccoons, and a host of other creatures also suffer similar fates. However, their deaths usually do not
cause injury or death to drivers or damage to vehicles, so they
generally receive much less attention.

Can anything be done to save some of these smaller animals?
Yes, to some extent, many of the suggestions for reducing deer-
vehicle collisions also can be used to avoid hitting other wildlife
on roads. Certainly, drivers can slow down when they see a confused animal ahead of them attempting to cross a road!

Urban Wildlife

More and more urban and suburban Americans are encountering
wildlife around their homes. Sometimes this is willingly, as when
bird feeding stations are established in backyards, or when backyard wildlife refuges are established. Successful, major and very
expensive efforts also are in progress to encourage endangered
Peregrine Falcons to nest on ledges or roofs of tall buildings and
tall bridges in urban areas. Baltimore, New York and Philadelphia
are among the American cities in which these magnificent falcons
are again nesting after suffering several decades of DDT-caused
breeding failures. Other raptors, including American Kestrels and
Barn Owls, also nest in some locations in urban and suburban
areas. All of these animals are welcome additions to urban living.

At other times, however, city dwellers unwillingly encounter
wildlife as when squirrels, Skunks, Raccoons, or other creatures
accidentally get into homes and must be removed humanely. The
topic of urban wildlife management is very important to wildlife
advocates. The Humane Society of the United States (HSUS) has

fact sheets, and a book regarding humane control of "nuisance" wildlife. Write to Data and Information Services, HSUS, 2100 L Street, NW, Washington, DC 20037.

Here are some basic steps that urban and suburban residents can take to avoid experiencing, or to cope with, unwanted wildlife:

🐾 Keep doors leading outdoors closed. It's easy for wildlife to enter buildings if doors remain open!

🐾 Tightly fasten lids on garbage containers to prevent raccoons from becoming accustomed to backyard food sources and perhaps entering houses or other buildings. If possible, keep sealed garbage containers indoors until collection day.

🐾 Install chimney caps to prevent wildlife from building nests inside these structures. It may be necessary to check with your local fire department for information regarding approved types of chimney caps.

🐾 Repair holes in roofs to prevent squirrels or other wildlife from entering buildings. Be sure, however, that wildlife is not trapped inside the building before repairs are done.

🐾 Be certain that adequate covers are in place over exhaust vents to prevent wildlife from entering buildings via these openings. Also repair broken windows and ripped screens.

🐾 Install adequate barriers or seals across openings beneath buildings to prevent wildlife from building dens there.

🐾 If a mouse, or another species of wildlife, is found indoors, use non-lethal live traps to remove them. Transport the animals a mile or more away from the building to prevent their return.

🐾 If a bat is found indoors, wait until it clings upside down to a drape or other object. Then carefully slip a large, wide-mouth bottle or other clear container over the animal, trapping it inside. Next, slip a stiff piece of cardboard underneath the mouth of the container and the bat, thus trapping the bat inside the container. Then, holding the cardboard tightly over the container so the bat can't escape, carry the animal outside and release it.

🐾 In many urban and suburban areas, Rock Doves (pigeons) roost and nest on ledges of tall buildings, in openings near the tops of buildings, under bridges, and in similar locations. Many of these places can be screened to prevent these birds from using them, thus avoiding "pigeon problems" in those locations. In addition, never feed feral Rock Doves in urban and suburban areas.

🐦 If very large Rock Dove populations exist in a city, encourage municipal officials to use Ornitrol as a fertility control technique. It is one of the few compounds registered and approved for use by the U.S. Environmental Protection Agency. Approximately 10 bags (30 pounds per bag) of Ornitrol are needed to deal with 400 doves, or 1,000 bags per 40,000 birds. One 30 pound bag of Ornitrol treats 40 Rock Doves for one day. For additional information, write to: Avitrol Corporation, 320 S. Boston, Tulsa, OK 74103.

🐦 In areas where Black Bears are found, never feed them! Many suburban Black Bear problems occur because well-meaning people feed these animals which then become habituated to people and depend upon the human food supply.

🐦 In many urban and suburban areas, migratory songbirds fly into large plate glass windows and are injured or killed. The problem can be serious and no entirely satisfactory solution is available. Part of the problem centers around the reflective surfaces of these windows. Reducing or eliminating reflective window surfaces also reduces the numbers of songbirds likely to strike windows and kill themselves. The following may be helpful solutions to the problem:

• Stretch fine netting across plate glass windows to prevent birds from hitting these large reflective surfaces.

• Place large images of hawks or owls on windows to frighten songbirds away from the windows.

• When designing new houses or other buildings, ask that large plate glass windows be tilted slightly downward to reduce the reflective surfaces of windows.

• Whenever possible, try to install plate glass windows that have minimum reflective surfaces.

• As glass manufacturers and contractors become aware of the problem of songbirds striking windows, new glass products may become available. Inquire if such items are available and how they can be used in new buildings and in structures being renovated.

7

What's Wrong With Hunting?

H unting is the most entrenched activity associated with wildlife, steeped in tradition, and strongly supported by political
and legal establishments. For protection advocates, hunting is the
most difficult of wildlife problems. Nevertheless, prohibiting hunting is a major priority. Although the number of hunters is declining, it will take decades of effort by those who set aside wishful
thinking to understand how to defeat legislative and regulatory
systems that protect hunting.

Nevertheless, activists opposing hunting are using a wide range
of tactics, but there is considerable difference of opinion regarding
the best methods of increasing wildlife protection. Meanwhile,
most wildlife organizations in the United States take one of three
positions regarding hunting:

🐾 They normally do not become involved in the hunting issue,
not viewing it as a major concern. The Sierra Club is such an organization, even though John Muir, its founder, opposed hunting.

🐾 They do not oppose hunting unless it threatens a species. The National Audubon Society is an example.

🐾 They support hunting. The National Wildlife Federation is one such organization, although many of its members seem not to be aware of that fact.

The many conflicting viewpoints among wildlife organizations clearly make the task of eliminating hunting quite difficult. If action is to be effective, it is important to examine some of the basic hunting issues.

What's Wrong With Hunting?

What's wrong with hunting? That's the most commonly asked wildlife question by the American public, let alone hunters, because about 16 million adult Americans still participate in hunting. Here are some answers:

🐾 *Hunters Enjoy Killing Wildlife.* Most hunters deny they enjoy killing claiming they hunt mostly to enjoy the outdoor experience and companionship with hunting friends. Nevertheless, other statements made by hunters refute that denial. Consider the following facts:

• Hunters, wildlife agencies and outdoor writers avoid stating that hunters kill animals for recreational purposes and that millions of birds and animals wounded by bullets or arrows suffer lingering pain before dying. Instead, hunters use a deceptive term and state that they "harvest" wildlife.

• One Pennsylvania deer hunter stated, "We outdoorsmen do not want to be civilized when we are hunting."

• Most "big game" hunters place great emphasis on killing "trophy" animals—generally the largest individuals, or those with the largest antlers.

🐾 *Hunting Is Effective and Humane.* The idea that hunting is humane contradicts established facts. Read Adrian Benke's *The Bowhunting Alternative* for a hunter's attack against archery hunting. Here are some appalling statistics:

• At one eastern Pennsylvania location, Mourning Dove

hunters slaughtered dozens of doves and numerous songbirds returning to a roosting site. None of these birds were retrieved. Their bodies were allowed to litter a nearby corn field in which they had been feeding.

• A Texas study reported that archers released 2,637 arrows to hit 258 deer, one deer being hit for every 11 arrows released, and one deer killed for every 21 arrows released.

• Bow hunting is extremely ineffective. It produces lingering suffering as wounded animals slowly bleed to death. A 1989 Texas study demonstrated that archers produce an approximately 50% deer crippling rate compared to a 7% crippling rate by gunners. Other studies confirm these statistics.

• Detailed information on the effectiveness of bow hunting was provided by Aaron N. Moen in the November 1989 issue of *Deer & Deer Hunting* magazine. Wildlife advocates will find that information useful in opposing bow hunting. For example, among hunter-killed deer in New York State, between 38 and 59% of the deer shot with arrows died within one minute of being hit (75% mortality rate within one minute for rifle hunters). However, when 98% of all deer hit with arrows were considered, it ranged between approximately 40 and 64 minutes for deer to expire. In some instances, death apparently took as long as 17 hours.

&. *Hunting Is Safe.* The idea that hunting is a safe activity for hunters and the general public is ridiculous. The danger to hunters and non-hunters is serious and continues year in and year out. Here are a few tragic examples of hunting-related deaths:

• On November 15, 1988, in one of the most famous involving fatal deer hunting accidents, 37-year-old Karen Wood, a mother of one-year-old twin girls, was shot to death in her suburban Maine backyard by a deer hunter. The hunter later claimed he thought Mrs. Wood's white mittens were the tails of running deer. The hunter was found innocent of manslaughter charges by a Penobscot County Superior Court jury.

• In November 1987, a 12-year-old turkey hunter in Florida fired at the sound of what he thought was a turkey and killed a 17-year-old hunter.

• In December 1987, a mother of five children was walking along a Pennsylvania village road when she was killed by a deer hunter's bullet. The hunter fled the scene of the accident.

• In September 1988, a hunter shooting Woodchucks on a Pennsylvania farm accidentally shot a teenager when his bullet passed through a farm building window.

• In March 1989, in the Pocono Mountains of eastern Pennsylvania, a nine-year-old boy allegedly pretending to be a hunter shot and killed a neighboring seven-year-old girl as she rode a snowmobile in her backyard. The boy was charged with murder as an adult in criminal court. Later the Pennsylvania Supreme Court halted the proceedings pending further oral argument. The legal maneuvers still are in progress regarding the appropriate court in which to deal with the case.

• In December 1989, a deer hunter hit a man in the leg as he was sleeping in his home in southeastern Pennsylvania. The hunter later was charged with recklessly endangering another person, failure to render assistance after an accident, and causing injury to a human being.

• In November 1990, Pennsylvania's small game hunting season began with the accidental shooting and killing of three turkey hunters. One of the hunters responsible for a death claimed he mistook a victim for a turkey! Each of the hunters was using a rifle equipped with a telescope.

• In November 1990, in an upper-class southeastern Pennsylvania community, a six-year-old boy carried his father's "unloaded" hunting rifle from the family car into their home after his father's return from a five-day hunting trip. Moments later the boy accidentally shot his two-year-old brother in the head. The little boy died a short time later in the hospital. The next day, area newspapers reported that the six-year-old "thinks his brother will be home any minute," indicating the boy does not understand he killed his brother.

As more and more land is developed, hunting inflicts increasing danger upon urban and suburban residents. Every year, innocent people are shot, injured or killed in their own yards, along roads or even asleep in bed. All of these tragic cases are unnecessary! It's time for the public to speak up!

🐾 *Hunters Ignore the Law*. Hunters frequently ignore wildlife laws. Aware of this fact, state wildlife agencies have established SPORT (Sportsmen Policing Our Ranks) programs in an effort to induce hunters to improve their attitudes and behavior. Nevertheless, poaching and other violations of wildlife laws are increasing. Consider these facts:

• During 1987, there were 128 assaults against 9,183 federal and state wildlife law enforcement agents, producing 28 injuries and two deaths. The likelihood that assaults on wildlife agents will be fatal are nine times higher than assaults on city police. In 1988, a United Press International report from Raleigh, NC, stated that attacks on wildlife law enforcement agents are increasing.

• In 1986, federal wildlife law enforcement agents raided a Long Island, New York, taxidermist's home and found 294 protected migratory birds mounted and for sale. Included were an endangered Peregrine Falcon, a Bald Eagle, 18 Merlins, 15 American Kestrels, 29 Barn Owls, 24 Long-eared Owls, and a number of egrets, herons, waterfowl, and other species.

• In 1988, the U.S. Fish and Wildlife Service completed a three-year undercover investigation of commercial hunting activities in Texas, arrested 22 people, and indicated as many as 200 people would be charged with criminal violation of waterfowl hunting regulations. More than 1,300 wildlife law violations were documented.

• On October 23, 1989, during one 12-hour period, 19 federal and Pennsylvania state wildlife agents checked 100 waterfowl hunters near Sunbury along the Susquehanna River to enforce steel shot regulations. They discovered a range of illegal activities, issued 22 citations and 25 warnings. Illegal activities included killing protected grebes, cormorants, American Black Ducks, exceeding bag limits, lead shot being used, lack of required federal duck stamps and shooting from boats under power.

• In 1990, Pennsylvania hunters were fined $1.5 million for wildlife violations. In all, 8,368 people were prosecuted and

12,152 issued warnings. Included were 716 spotlighting violations, 461 littering arrests, 392 unlawful taking, possession or transportation of game, 361 failing to tag big game properly, 332 spotlighting with a firearm in the vehicle, 230 hunting within a safety zone, 230 driving with a loaded firearm in the vehicle, 203 hunting, killing, or attempting to kill game during closed hours, and 112 hunting wildlife with bait or enticement.

• Kit Howard Breen, writing in *The Canada Goose*, suggests that much illegal waterfowl hunting by members of Congress and other Washington officials is ignored by officials of the Department of the Interior. She also states that law enforcement agents seeking to do their duty and who have arrested Congressmen and other ranking officials have been disciplined with transfers to areas outside the Chesapeake Bay region. Some are even threatened with dismissal.

• Illegal hunting in American national parks, where hunting is prohibited, is directly responsible for the loss of some of our nation's most spectacular wildlife treasures including Black Bears, Grizzly Bears, Dall Sheep, Elk, Gray Wolves and Golden Eagles. In 1988, for example, more than 2,000 "wildlife violations" were reported in our national parks. Financial gain is the primary motive behind this most illegal hunting.

• Poaching is rampant among American hunters (and hunters elsewhere in the world) as more wildlife habitat disappears. As outdoor newspaper and magazine writers continually put emphasis on trophy hunting, poaching is increasing alarmingly. According to the *New York Times*, New York State wildlife officers believe as many as one-third of the state's annual deer hunting kill is taken by poachers.

• Hunting from roads is a common illegal activity in many states. In 1990, in West Virginia, where road hunting is widespread, state wildlife law enforcement agents used a remote-controlled deer decoy to catch road hunters. In one three-week period, more than 120 road hunting violators were arrested and prosecuted—with a 100% conviction rate. In Pennsylvania, however, where deer decoys were used by agents, convictions of several road hunters were reversed by a Westmoreland County judge who ruled that a stuffed deer failed to meet the state's legal definition of wildlife, and that shooting a decoy was not hunting.

• Poaching information secured by special agents of the U.S. Fish and Wildlife Service, published in *Endangered Species UPDATE*, indicates that prices paid for illegally obtained wildlife, and wild animal and plant parts, are astounding. The following are representative examples.

Bald Eagle $2,500	Rhinoceros Horn $12,500 (per pound)
Peregrine Falcon $10,000	Siberian Tiger Skin $3,500
Gyrfalcon $120,000	Cockatoos $2,000
Grizzly Bear $5,000	Snow Leopard $14,000
Grizzly Bear claw $2,500	Mountain Gorilla $150,000
Polar Bear $6,000	Panda $3,700
"Grand Slam" Sheep $45,000	Ocelot $40,000 (per coat)
Mountain Goat $3,500	Imperial Amazon Macaw $30,000
Saguaro Cactus $15,000	Tiger Meat $130 (per pound)

• According to the *New York Times*, Black Bears (and bears in general) are declining worldwide and becoming especially vulnerable because of worldwide poaching to fill the demand in traditional Oriental (China, Japan and Korea) medical desires for bear parts such as gallbladders and claws.

• Poaching is a serious threat to the wildlife of East Africa, India and many other nations. Ecotourists also have been attacked and murdered by poachers in Kenya's national parks.

• The National Fish and Wildlife Forensics Laboratory was established by the U.S. Fish and Wildlife Service to assist agents in the battle to curb poaching and illegal traffic in wildlife.

• Wildlife advocates can help reduce the rise in poaching by reporting hunting license numbers, vehicle license numbers, and other related information. However, poachers are armed and dangerous and should not be challenged directly. Report them to enforcement officers.

🐾 *Hunters are Slobs.* The vast majority of hunters are slobs. They ignore property rights, know almost nothing about nongame wildlife, little about game species, and are insensitive to the needs and desires of non-hunters who wish to protect all wildlife. They also cause considerable damage to private property. Consider the following:

• Trespassing and Littering. Hunters are notorious trespassers and litterers.

• Killing Domestic Animals. Hunters carelessly shoot and kill cows, horses and other domestic animals instead of deer. These domestic animals are often shot close to occupied buildings and well within marked safety zones in which hunting is prohibited.

• Vandalism. In 1988, a man dumped 20 deer legs in a Butler County, PA, courthouse restroom — including some in the restroom plumbing fixtures! Countless roadsigns along rural roads also are peppered by shotgun pellets fired by hunters.

🦌 *Hunting Is A Sporting Activity*. There is nothing sporting about hunting — especially from wildlife's viewpoint. To participate in hunting, one must kill an unarmed, defenseless animal. Hunters are wildlife terrorists!

🦌 *Wildlife Exists for Human Use*. An assumption justifying sport hunting is that wildlife exists for human use. However, increasing numbers of people now reject that premise. They understand that all life forms, including people, are interrelated and part of complex but fragile ecological relationships and that no wild species exists for people's exploitation. Therefore, hunting has no justification.

🦌 *Hunters are Conservationists*. The claim that hunters are conservationists is a common misconception. Game animals are the major concern to hunters because they offer living targets for arrows and bullets. In order to produce as many game animals as possible to satisfy the hunters' demands, entire ecosystems are being altered. Predators, for example, routinely are shot and trapped in misguided efforts to increase game animal numbers. However, little or no concern is given to the ecological needs of other nongame species that also live on these lands. Thus the overall biodiversity of lands managed for wildlife is severely impacted.

🦌 *Hunting Prevents Deer from Starving*. A commonly held idea, repeatedly claimed by hunters, is that hunting prevents deer from starving to death. This is a deliberate attempt to misinform the public. Starvation is one of nature's natural methods of selectively reducing wildlife populations. Generally the very young, old, sick or weak animals starve, not the healthy individuals preferred by hunters.

Hunters Replace Predators. Another incorrect assumption often made by hunters is that they replace predators such as Mountain Lions and Gray Wolves that were exterminated by earlier generations of hunters. That's nonsense! Like starvation, predators generally kill weak, young, very old or expendable animals in wildlife populations — precisely the types of animals hunters avoid because they are not impressive trophies.

Hunters Pay for Wildlife Conservation. Much of the cost of game management programs, especially by the U.S. Fish and Wildlife Service, is paid by non-hunting American taxpayers rather than hunters as is commonly claimed. Most operating funds for state agencies comes from the sale of hunting and trapping licenses, fines and federal money derived from taxes on guns, ammunition and related equipment. Unfortunately, nongame species receive only a pittance of the funds devoted to wildlife programs. Thus demands of hunters seriously disrupt the needs of most wildlife species and produce distorted conservation programs inconsistent with the preservation of biological diversity.

Hunters Pollute the Environment. Federal regulations now require most hunters to use shells loaded with steel instead of lead pellets. However, early decades of hunting have caused lead pollution of wetlands, upland areas and other habitats. Large numbers of waterfowl, Bald Eagles and other aquatic bird life have been poisoned and killed by the accumulation of lead shot in wetlands food chains.

Hunting Increases Endangered Species. The increasing number of species being added to the endangered list is partly the fault of pro-hunting agencies that fail to respond to declining wildlife populations in time. If funds were poured into nongame programs, declines of some threatened species could be halted, or even reversed, before expensive crash programs are needed. Far too many endangered species such as Bald Eagles are shot and trapped illegally.

🐾 *Game Management Is A Scientific Activity.* Despite claims that game management is a scientific activity, its primary purpose is to produce game animals to use as hunting targets. Few conservation biologists regard game management as a valid activity. Indeed, disputes are increasing in the wildlife literature between managers and professional conservation biologists. The wildlife managers are sensitive to the activities of conservation biologists who seek to preserve biological diversity for ecological reasons. Game management, however, has little concern with an area's biological diversity.

Hunters Are Minority Wildlife Users

How important and widespread is hunting in the United States? It is necessary to consider background information regarding hunting and trapping in order to place proper perspective on these outdoor activities in America, particularly in major hunting states such as Alaska, Pennsylvania and Texas. Only then can the basic question be answered and effective ways developed to oppose hunting. Consider these facts:

🐾 Nationally, hunters represent only about 9% of the adult American population and that percentage is slowly declining. This tiny minority controls and regulates most wildlife programs in the United States.

🐾 In Pennsylvania, one of the strongest hunting states, a 1986 wildlife use survey conducted by the Wildlife Information Center indicated that only 14.5% of the population engaged in sport hunting (52.7% of the population, however, approved of hunting). A 1988 repeat of the survey again indicated 14.5% of the population engaged in sport hunting (and 54.5% of the population approved of hunting). In 1990, a statewide recreation survey conducted by the Commonwealth of Pennsylvania indicated that 15% of the population engaged in hunting.

🦌 Hunters (and fishermen) only pay for portions of state and federal wildlife programs via purchase of hunting, fishing and trapping licenses and taxes paid on the purchase of guns, ammunition and other equipment. However, the overwhelming portion of all of those programs is devoted to game species management.

🦌 Wildlife advocates need to provide significantly more funding to wildlife agencies and organizations so that programs devoted to the welfare of nongame wildlife will surpass those of game species. In other words, most wildlife users, including bird watchers and photographers, need to pay their share of wildlife conservation activities. To date, they are not doing so. Thus they allow an outspoken hunting minority to dominate wildlife programs and policies.

Hunter Harassment Laws

During recent years, approximately 38 states have enacted "hunter harassment" laws. A hunter harassment bill also is pending in Congress. The objective of these laws is to silence anyone from opposing hunting. However, hunter harassment laws in Connecticut and Wisconsin were ruled unconstitutional in court tests and the New Hampshire Supreme Court ruled a pending hunter harassment bill unconstitutional. The bill was dropped. Legal challenges of these laws doubtless will occur in other states in the near future.

Increasing numbers of wildlife advocates concerned about the hunter harassment issue are beginning to take actions. Various members of the Fund for Animals in several states are having small numbers of people arrested in violation of certain harassment laws. Here are some additional actions you can take to challenge hunter harassment legislation:

🦌 Write to your U.S. Representative or Senator expressing opposition to all hunter harassment bills. Mention your First Amendment rights and that you value your freedom of speech far more than legal guarantees to hunters.

🦌 In states with active hunter harassment laws, contact your state Representative or Senator and seek introduction of a bill to repeal such laws.

🐾 If you are an activist, join public demonstrations against hunter harassment laws.

🐾 Some individuals may wish to force the issue and challenge the legal validity of these laws. The Fund for Animals is the most active organization engaged in these test cases. They do this by birdwatching close to hunters on public lands, rustling leaves as they walk, or talking loudly. After being arrested for harassment, offenders contest the law in appropriate courts. However, there are serious risks and financial expense involved in this type of action. One person was jailed after she refused to pay a fine.

🐾 Before attempting to test hunter harassment laws, seek expert legal advice. One source may be the Rutgers University Animal Rights Law Clinic. If you are involved in a serious hunter harassment case, telephone the Clinic at (201) 648–5989 for more information.

Deer Hunting

To wildlife advocates, deer hunting is probably the most annoying of all hunting issues. Hundreds of demonstrations have been held through the United States in efforts to stop deer hunts – especially at state parks in suburban areas and at various wildlife refuges. Most of these efforts failed, but they have produced some positive results:

🐾 Demonstrations have received considerable media coverage and increased public awareness about the issue of deer management.

🐾 More people are becoming interested in deer and other wildlife issues through public exposure of hunting disputes.

🐾 Wildlife agencies are on notice that their traditional "good old boy" attitudes, programs and policies are no longer acceptable to a growing number of citizens.

🐾 State wildlife agencies will be pressured to add women and minority representatives to their commissions and non-hunters and even anti-hunters as staff employees. In short, the agencies will be pressured to become much more responsible to the general public instead of the hunter minority that now occupies most of their attention.

🐾 Nonlethal methods increasingly are being demanded for use in deer and other wildlife management. Among the important methods are the use of Swareflex roadside reflectors to reduce deer-vehicle collisions, fertility control vaccines in relatively small ecological islands such as many urban parks and establishment of inviolate wildlife refuges.

Bear Hunting

Black Bear hunting in America is becoming commonplace for a variety of reasons including the following:

🐾 Bears are forced to live in worsening habitats because of land development and highway construction; therefore, these large carnivores increasingly come into contact with people.

🐾 Complaints from farmers about Black Bear crop damage is increasing and are used by state agencies to justify bear hunting.

🐾 As more bear habitat is lost to development, former urban residents (who generally know little about wildlife) living in new suburban housing developments commonly and inappropriately feed bears. The animals become dependent upon human food offerings and if the food supplies disappear, they become hungry "pests."

🐾 Black Bear management is a factor increasing bear populations in some states such as Pennsylvania. Some bears have been trapped and transferred by the Pennsylvania Game Commission to increase bear populations in areas with small or no bear populations, thus broadening the distribution of these animals in the state for hunting purposes.

🐾 As hunters seek animals to kill in a shrinking habitat, the sale of hunting licenses declines and "bear complaints" increase, wildlife agencies increasingly are promoting bear hunting.

🐾 In Pennsylvania, the Game Commission seeks to have more

than 2,000 bears killed annually during the short hunting season. The result is that as many as 93,000 Black Bear hunters annually kill between 1,000 and 2,200 of the state's estimated 7,500 to 8,000 bears.

Not everyone, however, is pleased. Wildlife advocates are especially outraged and many others are speaking out against it. The result is that continuing disputes have developed. Here are some examples:

🐾 As many as 59 Black Bear cubs, including some females with cubs, have been killed in Pennsylvania during recent bear hunting seasons.

🐾 Some wildlife activists are seeking major revisions of Pennsylvania's Game Code so that bear hunting seasons do not begin until December, when female bears with cubs are already denned up.

🐾 Black Bear poaching can be expected to increase.

🐾 Recommendations have been made for the establishment of Black Bear sanctuaries in Pennsylvania, including state parks, natural areas in state forests and other wilderness areas. These recommendations are inconsistent with the Game Commission's desire to promote increased bear hunting.

🐾 At least one hunter was shot and killed while chasing a bear.

🐾 Some people eating undercooked Black Bear meat from the Pocono Mountains have contracted trichinosis, a parasitic illness.

🐾 In 1990, representatives from the Fund for Animals attempted to challenge Pennsylvania's "hunter harassment" law by disturbing Black Bear hunters in the Pocono Mountains. No arrests were made, however, thus preventing the activists from testing the law in court.

🐾 In California, the Fund for Animals sued the California Department of Fish and Game and was temporarily successful in stopping California's bear hunting season on the ground that the state wildlife agency lacked adequate information to accurately determine the size of the state's bear population and thus had no responsible basis for allowing bear hunting. Recently, however, the agency gathered new information and the ban on bear hunting was lifted.

🐾 Non-hunters and wildlife photographers wishing to observe or photograph Black Bears in their natural habitats are denied opportunities each time a bear is killed by a hunter.

Bison Hunting

Prior to the arrival of Europeans in North America, 50 million Bison populated the Great Plains and other areas. Moreover, for thousands of years American Indians lived in close harmony with these animals, hunting small numbers to satisfy their essential needs.

As the frontier pushed westward, however, the U.S. Army (aided by private market hunters) began a systematic extermination of Bison, thus depriving Plains Indians of their lifeblood. By late in the last century, fewer than 600 wild Bison survived. At the last moment, a few concerned conservationists began emergency actions to save these animals from extinction. As a result, a few thousand wild Bison live in western locations, including several thousand in Yellowstone National Park. Therein rests an increasingly complex and volatile problem, especially regarding park Bison. Consider the following facts:

🐾 Gray Wolves and other predators that normally play major roles in providing regulatory controls on large mammal populations such as Bison were exterminated in the Greater Yellowstone ecosystem earlier in this century. However, small numbers of wolves are naturally returning to the area and the National Park Service currently is making efforts to reintroduce wolves into Yellowstone National Park (see chapter 3 for details about the economic importance of wolf watching activities).

🐾 Bison herds within Yellowstone National Park (where hunting is prohibited) are increasing. During early winter, small numbers stray from the confines of the park and move onto adjacent cattle rangeland in Montana.

🐾 Some land within the Greater Yellowstone ecosystem outside the national park is where herds of cattle are grazed. Additional land within the ecosystem is federal land reserved as national forest. The result is that the Greater Yellowstone ecosystem has been fragmented and the natural movement patterns of Bison in the area are altered and sometimes severely disrupted.

🐾 Montana wildlife officials and cattle ranchers claim that brucellosis-infected Bison leaving Yellowstone National Park pose a serious threat to cattle. These people want infected Bison killed even though no cattle actually have contracted brucellosis.

🐾 Using that weak justification, Montana wildlife officials have established a limited Bison "hunting" season and issued a few hunting licenses for the slaughter of Bison wandering immediately outside the park.

🐾 The slaughter of habituated Bison, by gunners at close range, has erupted into a major dispute between wildlife advocates, Montana wildlife officials and hunters and National Park Service officials. The Fund for Animals is particularly involved in this issue and holds annual public demonstrations and protests against Bison killing directly beside gunners killing the Bison. The Fund correctly claims:

• Killing these magnificent animals has no ecological basis.

• Shooting park Bison at close range is similar to shooting a cow at 10 feet and is therefore a slaughter.

• No cattle grazing on lands adjacent to Yellowstone National Park have ever been infected by brucellosis from Bison living in the park.

To address this issue, in May 1990 the National Park Service issued a report entitled *Yellowstone Bison: Background and Issues* which contained an *Interim Management Plan* whose objectives are:

🐾 To reduce potential transmission of brucellosis from park Bison to cattle in the area adjacent to the park.

🐾 To reduce potential conflicts between people and property damage caused by Bison outside the park.

🐾 To ensure opportunities to observe free-ranging Bison in Yellowstone National Park.

🐾 To maintain a self-sustaining Bison population within the national park.

The park service offered the public opportunities to comment on the report and interim management plan. The Wildlife Information Center, for example, submitted the following recommendations to Yellowstone National Park officials:

🦬 Allow no Bison hunting within the national park, or on public or private lands adjacent to the park.

🦬 Allow Bison to roam anywhere within the Greater Yellowstone ecosystem.

🦬 Use fertility control when possible on Yellowstone's Bison herd.

🦬 Introduce the Gray Wolf into the Greater Yellowstone ecosystem.

🦬 Expand the borders of Yellowstone National Park to conform more closely to natural ecosystem borders. This means transferring some adjacent national forest lands to the National Park Service, with the full cooperation of the Secretaries of Agriculture and Interior, and perhaps Congress and the White House.

However, in December 1990, the Associated Press reported that Montana wildlife officials and the National Park Service announced that future Bison hunts would be modified so that the public understands the purpose is to keep Montana cattle herds free of brucellosis. State wildlife wardens and national park rangers would join private hunters in killing Bison wandering outside the national park.

Wildlife protection activists can comment on the Yellowstone National Park Bison hunting issue by mailing comments to: Bison Management Plan, National Park Service, P.O. Box 168, Yellowstone National Park, WY 82190.

Regretfully, an increasingly controversial proposal for a hunt of the world's largest Bison herd (4,000 animals) in Canada's 17,300-square-mile Wood Buffalo National Park also is being recommended by veterinary pathologists for the following reasons:

🦬 Proponents of the Bison hunt claim there are 3,500 animals infected with brucellosis and tuberculosis.

🦬 The genetic composition of Bison in Wood Buffalo National Park represents a mixture of Bison gene pools because animals from many North American locations were introduced into the park.

🐾 After elimination of the entire herd of diseased Bison, another disease-free herd of genetically pure Bison would be reintroduced.

However, public opposition to the hunt is growing and receiving international media coverage. The main reasons for opposing the Bison hunt include the following:

🐾 The issue of Bison health is "contrived" to make way for Bison ranching by local farmers who would then sell Bison and other wildlife raised on ranches for meat.

🐾 The validity of some of the scientific basis for the hunt is questionable.

🐾 There is little visual evidence of many diseased animals. The disease issue is greatly overstated.

🐾 It is impossible to track down and kill every individual Bison in the huge park.

🐾 There are covert plans to reduce the size of Wood Buffalo National Park, thus creating the need to eliminate so many Bison.

🐾 Because Wood Buffalo National Park is designated by UNESCO as a World Heritage site, an independent study should be made of the matter before any Bison are killed.

Like the Bison hunt issue at Yellowstone National Park in the United States, this Canadian issue will continue. Canadian wildlife advocates should voice their concerns.

Mourning Dove Hunting

Mourning Doves are among the most common migratory birds in North America, with overall autumn populations estimated at 475 million birds. To many people, doves represent symbols of peace. However, depending on the state where one lives, these birds can be classified either as gamebirds or songbirds. That means that doves are hunted heavily in many states, where dove hunting is the subject of continuing disputes between hunters and wildlife advocates and protected as songbirds in other states. The following are some of the reasons why activists object to Mourning Dove hunting:

🐾 Lead shot from Mourning Dove hunters has rapidly and seriously contaminated the fields with toxic lead in which dove hunting occurs regularly. Spent lead shot can increase by as much as 400% in fields where dove hunting takes place and remains available near the surface of the field until the land is tilled. Availability of spent lead shot on the surface of fields represents a food chain contamination risk to Mourning Doves and various other wildlife. For a summary of this problem, consult the *Wildlife Society Bulletin* (1989, 17 [2]: 184–189).

🐾 Mourning Doves have a low reproductive rate and a high mortality rate for nestlings.

🐾 Small numbers of Mourning Doves still are nesting in early September when the dove hunting seasons begin. Parents can be killed, resulting in the nestlings starving to death.

🐾 Mourning Doves are showing a serious long-term population decline in the seven states forming the Western Management Unit for this species by the U.S. Fish and Wildlife Service and in eastern states within the "Central Management Unit."

🐾 Mourning Dove hunters sometimes slaughter large numbers of birds and make no effort to retrieve the birds they shoot. The purpose of the dove hunters seems simply to kill wildlife for "enjoyment." In short, dove hunters are wildlife terrorists!

🐾 Public attitude surveys conducted in 1986 in California and Pennsylvania by the Wildlife Information Center demonstrated that 83.3% of Pennsylvanians opposed dove hunting, where 91.9% of Californians opposed Mourning Dove hunting.

The Committee for Dove Protection (69 E. Loop Drive, Camarillo, CA 93010, or 1221 Robin Hill, Rose Tree Road, Media, PA 19063) advocates that activists employ the following actions to oppose Mourning Dove hunting:

🐾 Maintain census records of Mourning Doves in your immediate area to determine if their populations are stable, increasing or decreasing.

🐾 Remain in contact with your state's wildlife agency and work to retain classification of the Mourning Dove as a songbird.

🐾 If Mourning Doves are considered gamebirds in your state, insist that these birds be reclassified as songbirds. If the latter effort is necessary, work with state legislators to introduce the necessary legislation.

🐾 Present outreach educational programs to various local clubs and other organizations regarding dove protection.

🐾 Discuss dove protection in public school biology classes, science clubs, etc.

🐾 Secure articles advocating Mourning Dove protection in local newspapers.

🐾 Employ a grassroots effort and discuss dove protection with people you meet.

Tundra Swan Hunting

The idea that Tundra Swans are gamebirds has emerged during recent years to the intense consternation of bird watchers, ornithologists, including Roger Tory Peterson and William J. L. Sladen, wildlife advocates and many others. Curiously, the National Audubon Society refuses to oppose Tundra Swan hunting.

Dr. Peterson, for example, stated: "I am very much disturbed by the proposal that the Tundra Swan may be included as a game species. This bird gives too many people pleasure to be sacrificed for the sport of a limited number of gunners. I am unconditionally opposed to the hunting of the Tundra Swan.

"I hope the Secretary of the Interior will acknowledge our point of view and recognize the recreational value of swans because of the number of people who like to see them alive and to watch them. The recreational and aesthetic value of the species is far greater than that in the name of sport."

The case against Tundra Swan hunting was well presented in a 1989 Wildlife Information Center report entitled *Tundra Swan Hunting: A Biological, Ecological and Wildlife Crisis* which formed the technical basis for the Center's petition to the U.S. Fish and Wildlife Service to ban all swan hunting in the United States. Despite the failure of that initial effort, increasing opposition to swan hunting is developing among animal rights organizations, internationally acclaimed swan researchers such as Dr. William Sladen, bird watchers and other conservationists.

Here are some of the confused justifications used by the U.S. Fish and Wildlife Service for promoting and allowing Tundra Swan hunting:

🐾 A desire for additional trophy hunting opportunities.

🐾 State and federal game biologists and managers claim there is a need to prevent agricultural and commercial shellfish damage due to swan feeding activities.

🐾 There is a desire to reduce the continental Tundra Swan population to between 60,000 and 80,000 birds despite there being no rational biological or ecological reason for selecting these figures.

🐾 Federal game biologists claim Tundra Swan hunting is necessary to prevent socioeconomic conflicts.

However, the Wildlife Information Center and various other wildlife protection organizations insist that Tundra Swan hunting causes a long list of serious and unjustified hardships to these magnificent birds. Consider these examples:

🐾 Swans suffer alteration of breeding behavior patterns, migratory behavior and ecological disruption of breeding, migratory and wintering populations.

🐾 The birds become more wary and changes can occur in use of migratory and/or wintering locations such as newly used sites.

🐾 Swan hunting causes emotional and social stress on bird watchers, wildlife photographers and non-hunters who look forward to seeing large flocks of wild swans.

🐾 Hunting diminishes swan viewing and photographic opportunities.

Therefore, the Wildlife Information Center recommends that all Tundra Swan hunting be banned. These birds offer exceptional wildlife-related recreation. Emphasis should be placed on non-killing activities such as bird watching, photography and wildlife tourism, all of which do not negatively affect swans if done correctly. More research also should be conducted to develop a range of nonlethal methods to reduce or eliminate crop damage caused by Tundra Swans.

Refuting Hunting Justifications

As more and more Americans openly speak out against hunting, it is important to provide solid rebuttals against pro-hunting arguments. Many already were presented in this chapter. Here are further ways to refute hunting:

🐾 ***Hunters Hunt to Enjoy the Outdoors.*** It is not necessary to kill wildlife to enjoy outdoor wildlife experiences. Millions of people participate in peaceful wildlife activities without killing animals. Examples are bird watchers, hawk watchers, whale watchers and nature photographers.

🐾 ***Hunters Need The Meat.*** A common argument used to justify hunting is that hunters need and use the meat to feed their families. However, examination of the costs in time and equipment necessary for successful hunting and the amount of meat secured, demonstrates that the cost per pound of the wild animal meat is much higher than the cost of meat purchased at a market. For example, it is estimated that a deer weighing 105 pounds yields only about 45 pounds of meat provided the animal was not severely damaged by the bullet and it was correctly field-dressed.

8

What's Wrong With Fur?

Trapping wild animals for their fur brings a painful death to millions of target animals, including ecologically important predators such as bobcats, coyotes and foxes, plus large numbers of nontarget animals, including Bald Eagles, other raptors and a wide assortment of mammals. It also disrupts wildlife communities by removing many important components of these ecosystems. That's why intelligent, and ecologically fashion-conscious people unconditionally condemn all uses of fur products—except, of course, when the original owners wear it.

Historical Perspectives

The long history of fur exploitation is complex and grotesque. Greta Nilsson provides an important summary of the trapping and fur trade business in *Facts About Furs* (Animal Welfare Institute) recommended to all wildlife advocates. Two additional books, *Furbearer Harvests in North America, 1600–1984* and *Wild Fur-*

bearer *Management and Conservation in North America* by Milan Novak and others (Ontario Ministry of Natural Resources and Ontario Trappers Association) also provide valuable insights into the staggering magnitude of the fur trade since the settlement of North America by Europeans several centuries ago. However, these two books are endorsements for the use of fur and attempt to justify wildlife trapping. Nevertheless, all three books detail a genuine wildlife holocaust. Consider these facts:

🐾 Fur trapping in North America began with the discovery and exploration of the continent by Europeans in the 1500s and early 1600s.

🐾 Early French Canadian colonies were established to exploit the fur trade and expand France's economy. Later Dutch and English settlers did the same.

🐾 The Hudson Bay Company, chartered in 1670, provided furs to England and controlled much of Canada's fur trade.

🐾 Predators were (and sometimes still are) widely considered "vermin" and destroyed whenever possible. Thus Gray Wolves, Mountain Lions, Black Bears and other predators were eliminated across most of their historic ranges.

🐾 Sea Mink were exterminated. The last individual was reported in 1880 in Maine.

🐾 Vast plains herds of Bison, once estimated at 50 million animals, were continually slaughtered until, by 1889, only 541 individuals remained.

🐾 From 1919 to 1921, some 99,693,380 wildlife pelts from North America, Europe, Russia, Australia and South America were sold. Included from North America, for example, were 2,540,971 Mink, 1,295,259 Red Fox, 1,094,502 Gray Wolves and Coyotes, 14,109,288 Muskrats, 1,713,000 Raccoons and 9,787,742 Opossums.

🐾 By the 1960s, public relations programs promoted "fun furs" and fur sales began increasing well into the 1980s. Only recently has the fur industry suffered a lack of public support, presumably because of anti-fur campaigns by animal rights advocates.

New Attitudes Toward Fur

Times and public attitudes are changing. Like hunting and trapping, the wearing of fur garments no longer is acceptable to more and more people in America and Europe. The results of anti-fur campaigns are measurable:

🐾 More furriers are suffering declining sales, declaring bankruptcy or going out of business.

🐾 During the period 1989–1990, *Newsday* reported that retail prices of fur products declined by some 25 to 35 percent.

🐾 During the 1990 Christmas season, some department stores discounted fur garments by 30 to 50 percent, offered 10 percent additional discounts and further offered zero percent interest for one year to fur garment buyers.

🐾 In Pennsylvania, a drastic decline in fur trapping activity has occurred in recent years. The Pennsylvania Trappers Association now promotes trapping as a "sport" rather than a means of earning a livelihood.

🐾 Anti-leghold trapping bills are being introduced in more state legislatures. Similar bills also are appearing at the county level.

🐾 Some mainstream charities are removing fur items from fund raising auctions because of the negative public image they generate.

Help Eliminate Uses of Fur and Trapping

Regretfully, the fur industry is not yet extinct. Nor does every anti-fur campaign produce positive results. In February 1990, for example, residents of Aspen, Colorado, voted on a proposal to ban fur sales in that trendy ski town. The proposed ban was defeated by nearly 2 to 1 after a bitter campaign that attracted national attention. Nevertheless, it is clear that a growing segment of the American public no longer wants anything to do with fur. It is only a matter of time before the fur industry collapses.

A wide range of actions are available to anyone wishing to participate in anti-fur campaigns:

🐾 ***Don't Buy or Wear Fur.*** First and foremost, never buy or wear fur products! Also encourage other members of your family, friends and neighbors to take similar action. The fur industry will collapse quickly if no market exists.

🐾 *Boycotts.* People opposed to the sale of fur products can use a very potent tactic to put pressure on stores that refuse to stop selling fur garments. Boycott those stores! Encourage other shoppers to do the same. Explain to uncooperative merchants the reasons for the boycott. When enough people stop buying at a store, owners will quickly pay attention.

🐾 *Donate Unwanted Fur Products.* If you own a fur coat, donate it to People for the Ethical Treatment of Animals (PETA), or another large organization conducting anti-fur campaigns. While they can't bring dead animals back to life, they use fur items for demonstration and educational purposes. Thus some positive benefits are derived.

🐾 *Demonstrations.* During recent years, in cities in America, Europe and elsewhere, public demonstrations opposing fur garments and leghold trapping have become a standard means of speaking out. On each Friday after Thanksgiving, for example, fur protests involving thousands of people are held in New York City, Chicago and other American cities. The impact of these protests, covered widely by the media, are resulting in diminished fur sales.

🐾 *Hand-out Literature.* Distribution of hand-out literature summarizing the problems with fur is a technique used by most animal rights activists. People for the Ethical Treatment of Animals, Animal Rights Mobilization (ARM), the International Society for Animal Rights (ISAR) and The Humane Society of the United States each have available free or inexpensive anti-fur and anti-leghold trap literature.

Some larger organizations also sell anti-fur kits. PETA, for example, has available a "Fur Is Dead" action pack and Friends of Animals sells T-shirts, buttons and a 10-minute "Faces Of Fur" videotape. The Humane Society of the United States also offers an anti-fur kit. Contact these organizations for lists of available items.

🐾 *Newspapers, Radio and Television.* At this point in anti-fur campaigns, countless newspaper articles, radio and television programs and news features have been presented regarding the public's growing opposition to the use of fur products. Activists should continue seeking additional coverage as a means of countering paid advertising from fur shops and department stores. In addition, don't forget letters-to-editors of newspapers.

🐾 **Keep Fur And Trapping Out Of Schools.** As advocates of the use of fur and leghold trapping increasingly come under attack, some trappers are attempting to take their ecologically unsound messages into public school classes. If you are a public school teacher, or a wildlife advocate and are aware of trappers attempting to give voice in school classes, insist that school authorities also require that anti-fur information and videotapes be used in the same school programs.

🐾 **Ban Leghold Traps.** Banning the use of leghold traps is a slow and difficult process, but Florida, Rhode Island and New Jersey have banned these barbaric devices and other states are considering similar legislative actions. Large organizations, such as The Humane Society of the United States and PETA, maintain lists of the current status of anti-leghold trap legislation. Contact them for information regarding your state.

🐾 **Fake Furs.** Fake furs are readily available in many department stores and shops across America. For people who must wear coats that simulate real fur, the use of fake fur is an alternative. However, wildlife advocates consider fake fur undesirable because it causes confusion and perpetuates the idea that natural resources exist for human use rather than fostering the concept that people are part of nature and ecological processes. Moreover, fake furs are made from petrochemicals and have undesirable impacts upon the environment. Therefore, fake fur is also discouraged.

🐾 **Buy Wildlife-Friendly Products.** As pointed out in Chapter 3, an excellent way to protect wildlife is to only buy wildlife-friendly products. These are products whose raw materials and manufacture do not harm wildlife. Since many firms now offer them, watch for ads for wildlife-friendly products in magazines such as *The Animals' Agenda* (456 Monroe Turnpike, P.O. Box 345, Monroe, CT 06468) or *E/The Environmental Magazine* (P.O. Box 5098, Westport, CT 06881) then select items from those firms.

9

Saving Other Wildlife

P rotecting wildlife other than game species is another top priority. There's much to do! Most wildlife are nongame animals,
and many have declining populations in need of prompt attention.
Whales and dolphins, birds, predators generally, and many other
species all urgently need help. The call by wildlife advocates to
refocus efforts from game species to nongame wildlife management is to be heeded. Here are some important wildlife protection
opportunities:

Biodiversity Crisis

Of the many complex issues that concern wildlife advocates, none
is more important than the worldwide extermination of species in
recent decades as a result of burning and cutting of tropical rain
forests, wetlands destruction, forest fragmentation, hunting and

trapping, pollution, traffic for the pet trade, and other related problems.

As Scott Lewis points out in *The Rainforest Book*, in the moments it takes you to read this page, a 10-city-block area of tropical rainforest will be destroyed—roughly 55,000 square miles of these priceless Edens of biological diversity in one year. Little wonder that conservation biologists are so worried about the loss of biodiversity. A significant part of the living fabric of our planet is being lost in less than one lifetime! To learn more about the worldwide biodiversity crisis read E. O. Wilson's important book *Biodiversity* and Paul and Anne Ehrlich's informative book *Extinction*.

To gain perspective regarding human-caused wildlife extinction, a brief review of global bird extinction during the past 400 years is a vivid reminder of the urgent need to protect wildlife. Since the late 1500s, at least 166 kinds of birds have become extinct, and the crisis is continuing without abatement.

🐦 The first recognized bird species to become extinct, the Chatham Island Swan, entered the list around the year 1590. Sir Peter Scott stated that hunting by Polynesians, who arrived in New Zealand around the 10th century, was the most likely cause for the swan's extinction.

🐦 During the next century another eight birds became extinct, including the Burly Lesser Moa, Great Elephantbird, and the famous Mauritius Dodo.

🐦 During the 1700s, another nine birds joined the extinct list. They included the Rodrigues Blue Rail, Rodrigues Parrot, Rodrigues Little Owl, and Tahiti Sandpiper.

🐦 During the 1800s, bird extinction increased alarmingly and widely, becoming a continuing torrent. No less than 70 birds became extinct during that century. Included were the Kangaroo Island Black Emu, Oahu Thrush, Mascarene Parrot, Great Auk, Hawaiian Brown Rail, Labrador Duck and Cuban Red Macaw.

🐦 During this century, another 77 wild birds have joined the extinct list. These include the Guadelupe Caracara, Guadelupe Flicker, Chatham Island Bellbird, Carolina Parakeet, Laysan

Honeycreeper, Heath Hen, Pink-headed Duck, Laysan Rail, Wake Island Rail and Passenger Pigeon. Many more are expected to disappear as tropical forests are lost. Not since the abrupt disappearance of the dinosaurs has extinction of wild species reached the present speed and magnitude.

With the loss of each species, the rich fabric of life that is the glory of our planet is irreparably torn—the tragic legacy of human greed and stupidity.

Can the public's concern about wildlife slow the loss of wild species? The demands are apparent. What about other wild animal and plant species, not yet discovered and named by biologists? What are their prospects for survival within the next 50 years? The realistic answer is grim.

Albatross Declines and Japanese Long-line Fishing

According to *New Scientist*, a global decline in albatrosses is in progress. Australian biologist Nigel Brothers claims that hooked, 100-kilometer-long Japanese long-line fishing is to blame. Based upon observations on board Japanese fishing ships, he estimates a minimum of 44,000 of the magnificent birds become snared on long-lines annually. The largest of the great albatrosses, the Wandering Albatross, is most frequently hooked. Some victims remain alive for days with the hook in their throat, then die as the fishermen pull out the hook. Others escape but die later. Fortunately, some of the Japanese fishing fleet is beginning to modify its equipment to place suspended streamers above the bait area to prevent ensnaring the albatross. Nevertheless, Wandering Albatross numbers now are in sharp decline.

Dissection

Among animal rights advocates in particular, dissection of frogs and other animals in schools and professional labs is the focus of a campaign to eliminate all dissection. There are various reasons for this opposition:

🐾 Dissection is an obsolete teaching method used during the last century and is out-of-place in modern schools.

🐾 Dissection is unnecessary because alternative teaching methods are available, including wall charts, realistic models, computer software programs, improved textbook illustrations and other aids.

🐾 Dissection puts emphasis on the death of animals rather than instilling in students respect in the wonder of living wildlife, its communities and ecosystems.

🐾 Use of frogs, in particular, represents an unacceptable threat to these animals as worldwide amphibian populations continue to suffer drastic declines.

Student activists opposed to frog and other animal dissection can receive excellent assistance from The Animal Legal Defense Fund (1363 Lincoln Ave., San Rafael, CA 94901) which operates a Dissection Hotline (1–800–922–3764). They have available two informative booklets entitled *Objecting To Dissection/A Student Handbook* and *Objecting to Dissection/A College Students' Handbook*. These booklets provide an important plan for students objecting to dissection. It is important that these steps be understood and followed carefully because complex (and costly) legal issues can be involved in protesting dissection. However keep in mind that alternatives to dissection are available as discussed in those booklets.

Driftnets and Dolphins

Driftnets are deadly threats to marine wildlife. Now widely used by foreign tuna fishing fleets in the Pacific Ocean and beginning to appear in the Atlantic Ocean, these nets extend from 40 to 80 miles and capture everything that comes into contact with them. In effect, they act like gigantic vacuum cleaners. Dolphins are especially vulnerable to drowning in driftnets and huge numbers of them already have been lost.

However, in 1990, the Earth Island Institute and various other organizations successfully convinced several major tuna canners to purchase and sell only "dolphin safe" tuna. A complete list of "dolphin safe" tuna brands is available from the Earth Island Institute (300 Broadway, San Francisco, CA 94133).

Protecting Birds of Prey

Birds of prey, or raptors, are vital members of wildlife communities. As carnivores high in the food chain, they depend upon animal prey lower in the food chain. Thus, healthy wildlife communities and ecosystems have numerous birds of prey representing a wide diversity of species. That's why these birds are important indicators of the health of wildlife communities and ecosystems.

Fortunately, extermination campaigns that hunters, farmers and others waged against birds of prey earlier in this century no longer occur in the United States. Activists today do not have to spend days, weeks and months in hawk shooting blinds along Pennsylvania's famous hawk ridges to prevent the slaughter of migrating hawks as they did as recently as 1956. However, that's not to say that random, illegal shooting of birds of prey has yet stopped. In 1989, for instance, two Ospreys were shot by hunters at a state park in Bucks County, Pennsylvania.

Wildlife advocates can help deter raptor shooting by being alert to any discovery of illegal shootings. The Wildlife Information Center operates an informal Raptor Protection Patrol to assist wildlife enforcement agencies. It provides officials with any information it receives about illegal raptor shootings or raptors caught in leghold or pole traps, poisoned or otherwise injured or threatened by illegal activities at game breeding areas, farms, ranches, public hunting areas or elsewhere. When abuses are discovered, volunteers try to secure photographs of the injured or dead birds and make detailed notes regarding the episode. However, volunteers are not authorized to enter private property. Nor do they handle injured or dead birds unless they have appropriate state and federal permits.

Here's the type of helpful information that should be sent to the Wildlife Information Center (629 Green St., Allentown, PA 18102):

🐾 Name of volunteer, address and telephone number.

🐾 Date of observation or photograph.

🐾 Exact location of observation or photograph.

🐾 Species and number of each species, of raptor involved.

🐾 Type of abuse: shot, trapped, poisoned, etc.

🐾 Other pertinent available information.

Raptor Protection Patrol volunteers are not state or federal agents. They do not conduct investigations or make arrests. They merely support raptor protection, provide extra eyes for wildlife agents and pass helpful information along to authorities so that raptor protection laws can be more fully enforced.

Sea Turtles

Sea turtles are ancient, seriously endangered animals due to various human activities including the following threats:

🐾 Until recently, at least 44,000 sea turtles annually were caught and killed in shrimp nets used by shrimpers in United States waters.

🐾 The turtles are killed for their skins, which in some countries are used in the manufacture of shoes.

🐾 Oil spills.

🐾 Nesting beaches in Florida and elsewhere are threatened by development, recreational vehicles and sand-cleaning equipment.

🐾 Artificial lights along streets near beaches can dissuade females from coming ashore to lay eggs and can confuse young turtles, causing them to turn away from the ocean, cross streets and get run over.

Many conservation organizations are working to save sea turtles and to find solutions to some of the serious threats to their survival. Current possible solutions include the following:

🐾 The American shrimping fleet must use TEDS (turtle excluder devices) to prevent sea turtles from becoming trapped in shrimp nets.

🐾 Street lights should be turned off during the six-month breeding season along Florida beach communities where turtles come ashore to lay eggs and where young turtles attempt to return to the ocean.

🐾 Breeding beaches in Florida and elsewhere should be protected by establishing wildlife refuges at those locations.

Commercial and Research Whaling

One of the major wildlife protection issues of the latter half of this century is the continuing dispute regarding commercial and research whaling. While most nations now have stopped commercial whaling, Japan and a few other insensitive nations continue "research" whaling activities — a thinly veiled excuse to continue commercial whaling under a misleading name. Therefore, marine mammal activists oppose all whaling activities and continue working to achieve complete, worldwide protection for all cetaceans.

Traveling Animal Shows

Most of this book is devoted to saving wildlife in its natural habitat, but certain aspects of wildlife protection deal with animals in captivity. One of the most disgusting is the use of rare and endangered wildlife by traveling animal shows. Well over 1,400 such shows now roam across America visiting shopping malls, county fairs and other public gatherings where they offer the public opportunities to have children photographed holding young African Lions, Leopards and Tigers.

In July 1989, the Wildlife Information Center published a detailed report entitled *Wildlife In Traveling Animal Shows: An Examination and Critique* in which the following basic conclusions were presented:

🐾 Traveling animal shows exhibit a dismal record of concern for and use of, wildlife including endangered, threatened and exotic species.

🐾 The most serious problems include animal abuse, disruption of basic behavior patterns, suspected use of drugged animals, lack of humaneness, commercial exploitation, distorted educational values, unjustified production of animals by some zoos and commercial breeders and tragic disposal of old or unwanted animals to exotic game ranches where some animals are shot by so-called "big game" hunters.

🐾 Governmental authorities have not dealt adequately with this problem in the United States. Neither APHIS (a branch of the U.S. Department of Agriculture) nor the U.S. Fish and Wildlife Service seem especially concerned about the matter. In the latter case, the Service foolishly allows widespread use of captive bred endangered species including Leopards and Tigers.

🐾 The public generally remains unaware of the seriousness of the matter. Moreover, people who shop in malls that use traveling animal shows as attractions and have their children photographed holding young African Lions, Leopards, Tigers or other species help to perpetuate this type of harmful activity.

🐾 Shopping malls offer an assortment of excellent and educationally valuable promotional alternatives, including spectacular life-size dinosaur exhibits.

As a result of visits to shopping malls and the detailed information presented in its *Wildlife in Traveling Animal Shows* report, the Wildlife Information Center made the following recommendations:

🐾 Legislative or regulatory bans on traveling animal shows are necessary.

🐾 Government officials should clearly define traveling animal shows and promptly adopt bans on them. Denmark and Sweden already have banned or restricted this type of wildlife exploitation.

🐾 The Department of Agriculture and the U.S. Fish and Wildlife Service should exert more control regarding examination of permit applications.

🐾 Shopping malls should use alternative wildlife and nature exhibits and promotional programs such as conservation and nature poster exhibits, dinosaur exhibits, film and videotape mini-festivals, wildlife art exhibits, and wildlife and nature photography exhibits.

Eating To Save Wildlife

An important, but commonly overlooked, activity that everyone concerned about wildlife protection can do immediately is to change eating habits. One's daily diet can play an effective role in helping to protect wildlife without the need for new laws and regulations. Simply by eating lower on the food chain, activists can directly and immediately increase wildlife protection. Consider the following opportunities:

🐾 By stopping consumption of all beef, much less tropical rainforest will be cleared to provide cattle pasture.

🐾 Rangeland in the United States will be much less degraded and water pollution in major cattle raising areas also will be lessened.

🐾 Federal and state predator control programs designed to "protect" cattle and sheep from Gray Wolves, Coyotes, Mountain Lions, foxes and even eagles will be drastically curtailed or eliminated. That means increased wildlife protection for predators and drastically reduced uses of leghold traps and poisons such as Compound 1080.

🐾 Substantial reduction in cattle ranching will help to lower methane emissions, an important greenhouse gas and thus help to slow the global greenhouse effect.

🐾 By avoiding consumption of tuna and other fish, an activist lessens the impact upon wildlife including dolphins, seabirds and other marine species.

Wild Bird Pet Trade

When people think of pets they probably think of cats and dogs. Unfortunately, huge numbers of an enormous variety of wild birds (and other wildlife species) also are sold in pet shops throughout the world. This creates massive international traffic to supply the pet trade's demands. It also is directly responsible for the endangered status of some bird species, especially parrots and macaws and seriously depleted populations of other wild animals.

Wildlife advocates are attempting to secure federal legislation and certain treaty changes. CITES Appendix one, for instance, now lists dozens of endangered bird and other wildlife species and prohibits international traffic for each. As of mid-August 1990, a total of 109 nations were parties to CITES, making its treaty one of the world's most important wildlife protection tools. However, enforcement of restrictions required by CITES can be difficult, especially in third world nations and large numbers of endangered species destined for sale by pet shops still slip through ports-of-entry in many nations.

Wildlife smuggling nets about $1.5 billion annually worldwide according to CITES officials. A Black Palm Cockatoo or a Hyacinth Macaw can bring as much as $10,000 each on the black market and one ounce of endangered Black Rhinoceros horn is worth about $1,000. Illegal traffic in endangered wildlife is a lucrative business! Here is additional information about wildlife in the pet trade.

🐾 Entering tropical forests to cut down nest trees and rob eggs or nestlings of rare birds is one method the pet industry uses to secure birds for sale in American pet shops. Other capture methods include use of sticky lures, nets, traps and wing-shooting.

🐾 The pet industry's activities annually result in the inhumane deaths of millions of tropical birds during the capture, holding and exportation process.

🐾 More than 25% of wild birds exported to the United States routinely are dead upon arrival at our ports-of-entry.

🐾 Wild birds are shipped to the United States and other nations under appalling conditions. Hundreds of thousands more birds are dead at our ports-of-entry or are destroyed during the federal quarantine process because they are diseased, or pose a lethal threat to the poultry industry or public health. The pet industry, eager for quick and high profits, ignores these concerns and turns to tropical nations with inadequate legal enforcement of wildlife laws, to exploit spectacular tropical bird life.

🐾 The assault on tropical birds is a major wildlife conservation crisis.

🐾 Smuggling of tropical birds and other wildlife is now a major wildlife law enforcement task.

🐾 Hard drugs are included in some shipments of live wild birds.

🐾 Federal law prohibits *native* birds from being sold or used as pets in the United States.

🐾 Parrots and their relatives are documented carriers of *velogenic viserotopic* Newcastle disease (VVND), a major threat to the poultry industry and *psittacosis* which is also a human disease.

🐾 In 1971, in California, the poultry industry suffered a $56 million loss due to an epidemic of Newcastle disease transmitted from wild pet birds to poultry. Taxpayers paid most of that sum in industry compensation.

🐾 Most wild birds shipped to the United States are done so in crowded and inhumane ways lacking food or water.

🐾 Hundreds of millions of birds have been removed from the wild during this century for sale as pets throughout the world.

🐾 Most wild birds are not suitable pets.

🐾 A growing number of pet dealers have been convicted in federal courts for illegal smuggling of wild birds. According to an October 1990 report published in *Traffic USA*, which monitors international trade in wildlife and wildlife products, the Justice Department estimates that 150,000 exotic birds (mostly parrots) are smuggled annually into the United States from Mexico.

🐾 In one *Washington Post* story, rare non-Mexican birds seized by U.S. Customs and Fish and Wildlife Service agents at one Mexican-United States border point included Black Palm Cockatoos, Military Macaws and Hyacinth Macaws. The latter is one of the world's rarest birds and one of the largest and most spectacular parrots. In this particular smuggling episode, hundreds of birds of seven species were involved with a commercial value to the pet trade of about $500,000. Defendants in the case included a Mexican veterinarian, an American bird dealer and a bird broker according to the San Diego U.S. Attorney's office.

🐾 New York State's pioneering Wild Bird Law was twice upheld as valid by federal courts after the pet trade challenged the law.

🐾 Captive bred birds can adequately meet pet industry demands for birds and eliminate the need for capturing wild birds. Captive bred birds also are more suited as pets because of their more docile behavior and better health. Better still, do not buy any birds as pets.

The pet trade's massive international traffic in wild birds is tragic because sales of wild birds as pets are unnecessary and aggravating the global bird conservation crisis. According to an International Council For Bird Preservation world checklist of threatened birds, 1,000 (11%) of the world's approximately 9,000 wild bird species are threatened. Many are tropical birds jeopardized by the pet trade's activities. This is alarming because conservationists and government leaders are working to avoid the extinction of wildlife as a result of loss of tropical forests.

In Pennsylvania, a landmark Wild Bird Bill would have banned the importation for sale and sale of *wild* birds but allowed the sale of captive-bred birds, had the legislative effort been successful. This effort followed New York State's pioneering Wild Bird Law. Dozens of organizations and ornithologist/author Roger Tory Peterson endorsed the effort. Unfortunately, the pet trade created enough confusion among legislators to kill the bill. Therefore, now is the time for bird watchers and ornithologists to join wildlife advocates in securing enactment of a national Wild Bird Bill.

Wildlife and War

The effects of non-nuclear war on people and nations are horrific. However, relatively little nontechnical information is available regarding the effects of military activities upon wildlife and the environment. Nevertheless, wars have serious short and long-term effects upon wildlife and the environment. For example, a summary of effects of low-altitude military aircraft flights upon wildlife appeared in *Stopping Proposed Low-Altitude Military Aircraft Flights: A Pennsylvania Case Study* (Wildlife Information Center). Some other effects of war and other military activities upon wildlife and the environment include the following:

🐾 *Extinction of Species.* During the Second World War, American servicemen stationed on the island of Baltra in the Galapagos archipelago exterminated several native wildlife species on that island, including Galapagos Hawks, a mockingbird species and Land Iguanas.

🐾 **Indiscriminate Shooting of Wildlife.** During various wars in Africa, military troops indiscriminately shot and killed large numbers of mammals including African Elephants, Uganda Knobs, African Lions and Black Rhinos.

🐾 **Reduction or Elimination of Wildlife.** In some locations, military authorities deliberately engage in efforts to reduce or eliminate wildlife that cause problems. In the 1960s on Midway Atoll in the Pacific Ocean, the U.S. Navy destroyed at least 200,000 eggs of Laysan Albatrosses and other seabirds and killed (by clubbing and bulldozing) more than 50,000 adult and nestling albatrosses because the birds nest on the atoll. Metal paving also was placed over at least 50% of Sand Island's sand areas, where albatrosses had nested for thousands of years. This prevented large numbers of albatrosses from using former breeding sites. Important sand-holding vegetation also was removed by bulldozing, grading and surfacing operations. Destruction of the birds and their habitat was ordered because Midway is a naval air station, and there were collisions between military aircraft and albatrosses.

🐾 **Cetacean-Warship Collisions.** During the 1991 Persian Gulf War, at least three whales were killed after colliding with warships.

🐾 **General Habitat Destruction.** Destruction of wildlife habitat is always one of the products of war, regardless of where hostilities occur. During the 1991 Persian Gulf War, Iraq's release of huge amounts of oil into the Gulf caused massive pollution of the marine environment and the death of large numbers of birds and other wildlife. In the internationally important Snake River Birds of Prey Natural Area in Idaho, for instance, tank training activities also threaten habitat essential to a major concentration of raptors.

🐾 **Desert Ecosystem Destruction.** Use of tanks and other heavy equipment in desert battles or other military maneuvers has widespread, direct and indirect effects upon fragile desert wildlife and ecosystems. The equipment kills and maims ground-dwelling animals, seriously reduces the ability of desert wildlife to maintain adequately large populations, reduces or eliminates raptor and other predator populations, collapses retreat burrows used by mammals and reptiles, destroys nests of birds in shrubs and bushes, destroys vegetation by exposing and/or crushing roots, upsets desert soil water storage capacity and compacts soil. Camping and staging areas cause further serious damage to desert ecosystems. As a result, long periods are needed for deserts and their wildlife populations to recover from military damage. Tank tracks from World War II battles still remain visible in several North African deserts.

&. *Tropical Forest Destruction.* When civilians are displaced from their homes because of warfare, they can seriously damage sensitive environmental areas and wildlife habitats. After the invasion of Panama by American military forces, 30,000 displaced Panamanians moved into tropical forests and sensitive watershed areas near Panama City. Environmentalists estimate that approximately 175,000 acres of virgin tropical forest habitat eventually will be destroyed by these people. Similar destruction of rainforests by displaced people also is occurring in El Salvador and elsewhere in Central America.

&. *Equipment Litter.* In some battle areas, destroyed and abandoned military equipment remains on battlefields and litters the countryside. Closed or abandoned military installations also result in buildings, equipment and trash littering islands and mainland areas.

&. *Toxic Chemical Contamination.* Chemicals used as military weapons cause short- and long-term impacts upon people, wildlife and the environment. In Vietnam, large areas of tropical forests (vital wildlife habitat) were destroyed after being sprayed with chemicals such as Agent Orange. The long-term effects of these chemicals upon wildlife are largely unknown, but Agent Orange contains dioxins which can have a wide range of hazardous effects upon some wildlife species including mortality, and carcinogenic, mutagenic, teratogenic, reproductive and other effects.

🐾 *Other Chemical Contamination.* During military actions, leaks from sunken ships and other equipment can cause oil spills that can kill wildlife, pollute the environment and damage fragile areas such as coral reefs.

🐾 *Global Warming Effects.* During the 1991 Persian Gulf War, a scientific adviser to Jordan's King Hussein suggested that increased temperatures from burning oil wells and explosions could result in a 30-year speed-up of global warming. Massive quantities of greenhouse gases were released into the atmosphere as Kuwait's oil wells burned as a result of Iraq's use of ecocide during the Gulf War.

🐾 *Damage of Archaeological Ruins.* Secret 1988 United States military maneuvers in Guatemala damaged archaeological monuments in Yaxha not far from the famous pre-Colombian city of Tikal.

🐾 *Beneficial Effects of War.* Ironically, long-term effects of war sometimes can benefit wildlife! In Truk Lagoon in Micronesia, for example, sunken Japanese warships now support an artificial reef rich in corals, sponges and fishes. The demilitarized zone between North and South Korea is a wildlife sanctuary where endangered White-naped Cranes winter and populations of Tigers increased in Southeast Asia's tropical forests during the Vietnam War.

Despite any long-term war benefits to wildlife, what is the solution to the problem of war? Ban it! In addition to obvious benefits to people, efforts to save global biological diversity demand no less. Here are ways that activists can help to assure that military activities inflict minimal damage on wildlife and the environment.

🐾 *Elect Public Officials Critically.* When voting for the President of the United States and Members of Congress, examine each candidate's wildlife and environmental protection positions. Vote only for those who have acceptable positions and continually monitor their activities after being elected. If necessary, remind elected officials of their campaign promises.

🐾 *Write to Public Officials.* Write letters to public officials objecting to (or supporting) their wildlife protection activities.

🐾 *Monitor Federal Register Proposals.* Federal agencies are required to publish details of proposed activities affecting wildlife and the environment in the *Federal Register* (FR) which appears daily and is available in many public libraries. Activists monitoring Department of Defense activities that can affect wildlife should check each new issue for details of proposed activities and projects. Then prepare comments and mail them to the agency involved.

&. *Contact Military Officials.* Write directly to military officers seeking additional information regarding threats to wildlife on military bases or resulting from military activities. Do not accept vague and incomplete information.

&. *Freedom of Information Requests.* If military officers are uncooperative, use the Freedom of Information Act to secure the information. This technique sometimes is productive.

&. *Action Alerts.* When wildlife and conservation organizations issue action alerts, respond promptly with whatever help is requested. Action alerts are issued for important matters at critical times. A prompt response is important and necessary.

Chapter 10
WILDLIFE PROTECTION
ORGANIZATIONS

In the United States alone, there are more than 450 international, national and regional organizations involved in some way with wildlife. There also are additional state wildlife organizations. However, many of these groups are not opposed to hunting and trapping. Indeed, some actively (even avidly) support killing wildlife for recreational purposes. Nevertheless, quite a few either advocate wildlife protection or engage in activities that are important to the advancement of wildlife protection. Their names and addresses are listed here. They deserve the support of serious wildlife protection activists.

American Cave Conservation
Association
131 Main and Cave Sts.,
P.O. Box 409
Horse Cave, KY 42749

American Cetacean Society
P.O. Box 2639
San Pedro, CA 90731

American Horse Protection
Association, Inc
1000 29th St., NW, Suite T-100
Washington, DC 20007

American Humane Association
9725 E. Hampden
Denver, CO 80231

Animal Protection Institute
of America
P.O. Box 22505,
6130 Freeport Blvd.
Sacramento, CA 95822

Animal Rights Mobilization
P.O. Box 1553
Williamsport, PA 17703

Animal Welfare Institute
P.O. Box 3650
Washington, D.C. 20007

Bat Conservation International
P.O. Box 162603
Austin, TX 78716

Beaver Defenders
Unexpected Wildlife Refuge, Inc.
Newfield, NJ 08344

Bounty Information Service
Stephens College Post Office
Columbia, MO 65215

Center For Marine Conservation
1725 DeSales St. NW, Suite 500
Washington, D.C. 20036

Committee to Abolish Sport
Hunting
P.O. Box 43
White Plains, NY 10605

Cousteau Society, Inc.
930 W. 21st St.
Norfolk, VA 23517

Defenders of Wildlife
1244 19th St. NW
Washington, D.C. 20036

Earth Island Institute
300 Broadway, Suite 28
San Francisco, CA 94133

Elsa Wild Animal Appeal
P.O. Box 4572
North Hollywood, CA 91617-0572

Friends of Animals
P.O. Box 1244
Norwalk, CT 06856

Friends of the Sea Otter
P.O. Box 221220
Carmel, CA 93922

Fund For Animals
200 West 57th St.
New York, NY 10019

Greenpeace USA, Inc.
1436 U St., NW
Washington, D.C. 20009

Hawk Mountain Sanctuary
Association
Route 2, Box 191
Kempton, PA 19529

Humane Society of the United
States
2100 L St., NW
Washington, D.C. 20037

International Crane Foundation
E-11376, Shady Lane Road
Baraboo, WI 53913-9778

International Fund for Animal
Welfare
P.O. Box 193
Yarmouth Port, MA 02675

International Osprey
Foundation, Inc.
P.O. Box 250
Sanibel, FL 33957

International Primate Protection
League
P.O. Box 766
Summerville, SC 29484

Marine Mammal Fund
Fort Mason Center, Bldg. E
San Francisco, CA 94123

Mountain Lion Preservation
Foundation
P.O. Box 1896
Sacramento, CA 95809

National Speleological
Society, Inc.
Cave Ave.
Huntsville, AL 35810

Nature Conservancy
1815 North Lynn St.
Arlington, VA 22209

North American Bluebird Society
P.O. Box 6295
Silver Spring, MD 20906

North American Loon Fund
R.R. 4, Box 240C
Meredith, NH 03253

North American Wolf Society
P.O. Box 82950
Fairbanks, AK 99708

Planned Parenthood Federation
of American, Inc.
810 Seventh Ave.
New York, NY 10019

Primarily Primates
P.O. Box 15306
San Antonio, TX 78212

Rainforest Action Network
301 Broadway, Suite A
San Francisco, CA 94133

Rainforest Alliance
270 Lafayette St., Suite 512
New York, NY 10012

Save The Dolphins Project, Earth
Island Institute
300 Broadway, Suite 28
San Francisco, CA 94133

Save The Manatee Club
500 N. Maitland Ave., Suite 210
Maitland, FL 32751

Save The Redwoods League
114 Sansome St., Room 605
San Francisco, CA 94104

Sea Shepherd Conservation
Society
P.O. Box 7000-S
Redondo Beach, CA 90277

Society For Animal Protective
Legislation
P.O. Box 3719, Georgetown
Station
Washington, DC 20007

Tall Grass Prairie Alliance
P.O. Box 557
Topeka, KS 66601

Wild Canid Survival And Re-
search Center/Wolf Sanctuary
P.O. Box 760
Eureka, MO 63025

Wild Horse Organized
Assistance, Inc.
P.O. Box 555
Reno, NV 89504

Wildlife Conservation
International
New York Zoological Society
185th St. and South Blvd.,
Building A
Bronx, NY 10460

Wildlife Information Center, Inc.
629 Green St.
Allentown, PA 18102

Wildlife Refuge Reform Coalition
P.O. Box 18414
Washington, DC 20036–8414

World Society For The Protection
Of Animals
29 Perkins St., P.O. Box 190
Boston, MA 02130

Xerces Society
10 SW Ash St.
Portland, OR 97204

Zero Population Growth
1400 16th St., NW, Suite 320
Washington, DC 20036

Chapter 11
SUGGESTED READING

Being well informed about wildlife issues is the first requirement for wildlife protection activists. Beyond information contained in this book, there is a wealth of information available in libraries. Periodicals containing wildlife protection information including *Animals' Agenda, Animals Magazine, E Magazine*, and many others commonly publish informative and useful articles featuring various aspects of the wildlife protection viewpoint. Other periodicals, not allied to (or necessarily sympathetic to) the wildlife protection viewpoint but containing information activists should know about, include *American Birds, Audubon, Buzzworm, Journal of Wildlife Management, Wildlife Society Bulletin*, and many others.

There also are numerous books pertaining to the varied and complex aspects of wildlife protection. Titles listed here include many on the Wildlife Information Center's "Wildlife Protector" HyperCard stack for Macintosh computers. Some of these books contain information that is objectionable to wildlife protection activists, but provide necessary background information. However, in one way or another, each book listed here is important to wildlife protection activists.

Animal Rights

Fox, Michael W. *Returning to Eden/Animal Rights and Human Responsibility*. Viking Press, 1980.

Fraser, Laura, et al. *The Animal Rights Handbook*. Venice, CA: Living Planet Press, 1990.

Regan, Tom. *The Case For Animal Rights*. Berkeley, CA: University of California Press, 1983.

Singer, Peter. *In Defense of Animals*. Harper & Row, 1985.

——. *Animal Liberation/A New Ethics For Our Treatment of Animals*. Random House, 1990.

Antarctic

Barnes, James N. *Let's Save Antarctica!* Universe Books, 1982.

Fraser, Conon. *Beyond the Roaring Forties/New Zealand's Subantarctic Islands. New Zealand: Government Printing Office Publishing, Wellington, 1986.

May, John. *The Greenpeace Book of Antarctica/A New View of the Seventh Continent*. Doubleday, 1989.

Murphy, Robert Cushman. *Oceanic Birds of South America*. Two volumes. American Museum of Natural History, 1936.

——. *Logbook for Grace*. Macmillan Co, 1947.

Neider, Charles. *Beyond Cape Horn/Travels in the Antarctic*. San Francisco: Sierra Club Books, 1980.

Parmelee, David F. *Bird Island in Antarctic Waters*. Minneapolis: University of Minnesota Press, 1980.

Peterson, Roger Tory. *Penguins*. Boston: Houghton Mifflin, 1979.

Stonehouse, Bernard. *Animals of the Antarctic/The Ecology of the Far South*. Holt, Rinehart and Winston, 1972.

Watson, George E. *Birds of the Antarctic and Sub-Antarctic*. Washington, DC: American Geophysical Union, 1975.

Arctic

Bruemmer, Fred. *Arctic Animals/A Celebration of Survival*. Minocqua, WI: NorthWord Press, 1986.

Crisler, Lois. *Arctic Wild*. Harper & Brothers, 1956.

Ketchum, Robert Glenn. *The Tongass/Alaska's Vanishing Rainforest*. Aperture, 1987.

Murie, Adolph. *A Naturalist in Alaska*. Devin-Adair Company, 1961.

Murray, John A. *A Republic of Rivers/Three Centuries of Nature Writing from Alaska and the Yukon*. Oxford University Press, 1990.

Watkins, T. H. *Vanishing Arctic/Alaska's National Wildlife Refuge*. Aperture, 1988.

Bats

Allen, Glover Morrill. *Bats*. Dover, 1939.

Hill, John E. and James D. Smith. *Bats/A Natural History*. Austin, TX: University of Texas Press, 1984.

Lollar, Amanda. *The Bat in My Pocket*. Santa Barbara: Capra Press, 1992.

Tuttle, Merlin D. *America's Neighborhood Bats*. Austin, TX: University of Texas Press, 1988.

Bears

Carey, Alan. *In the Path of the Grizzly*. Flagstaff, AZ: Northland Press, 1986.

Catton, Chris. *Pandas*. Facts On File, 1990.

Domico, Terry. *Bears of the World*. Facts On File, 1988.

Herrero, Stephen. *Bear Attacks/Their Causes and Avoidance*. Nick Lyons Books, 1985.

Miles, Hugh and Mike Salisbury. *Kingdom of the Ice Bear*. Austin, TX: University of Texas Press, 1985.

Mills, William. *Bears And Men: A Gathering*. Chapel Hill, NC: Algonquin Books of Chapel Hill, 1986.

Russell, Andy. *Grizzly Country*. Nick Lyons Books, 1967.

Schullery, Paul. *The Bears of Yellowstone*. Boulder, CO: Roberts Rinehart, Inc., 1986.

Biological Diversity

Fowler, Cary and Pat Mooney. *Shattering/Food, Politics, and The Loss of Genetic Diversity*. Tucson, AZ: University of Arizona Press, 1990.

Huntley, B. J. (Editor). *Biotic Diversity in Southern Africa/Concepts and Conservation*. Oxford University Press, 1989.

Myers, Norman. *The Sinking Ark/A New Look at the Problem of Disappearing Species*. Elmsford, NY: Pergamon Press, 1979.

Wilson, E. O. (Editor). *Biodiversity*. Washington, DC: National Academy Press, 1988.

Birds of Prey

Bijleveld, Maarten. *Birds of Prey in Europe*. London: Macmillan Press, 1974.

Brett, James J. *The Mountain & the Migration/A Guide to Hawk Mountain*. Kempton, PA: Hawk Mountain Sanctuary Assn., 1986.

Broun, Maurice. *Hawks Aloft: The Story of Hawk Mountain*. Dodd, Mead Co., 1949.

Brown, Leslie. *Eagles of the World*. Universe Books, 1976.

——. *Birds of Prey/Their Biology and Ecology*. A & W Publishers, 1976.

Brown, Leslie and Dean Amadon. *Eagles, Hawks and Falcons of the World*. 2 vols. McGraw-Hill Book Co., 1968.

Burton, John A. *Owls of the World*. E. P. Dutton & Co., 1973.

Cade, Tom J. *The Falcons of the World*. Ithaca, NY: Cornell University Press, 1982.

Cade, Tom J. et al. *Peregrine Falcon Populations/Their Management and Recovery*. Boise, ID: The Peregrine Fund, 1988.

Clark, William S. *A Field Guide to Hawks of North America*. Boston, MA: Houghton Mifflin, 1987.

Craighead, John J. and Frank C. Craighead, Jr. *Hawks, Owls and Wildlife.* Harrisburg, PA: Stackpole Company, 1956.

de la Torre, Julio, and Art Wolfe. *Owls/Their Life and Behavior.* Crown Publishers, 1990.

Dunne, Pete, David Sibley, and Clay Sutton. *Hawks in Flight.* Boston, MA: Houghton Mifflin Co., 1988.

Gerrard, Jon M. and Gary R. Bortolotti. *The Bald Eagle/Haunts and Habits of a Wilderness Monarch.* Washington, DC: Smithsonian Institution Press, 1988.

Heintzelman, Donald S. *Autumn Hawk Flights/The Migrations in Eastern North America.* New Brunswick, NJ: Rutgers University Press, 1975.

———. *Hawks and Owls of North America.* Universe Books, 1979.

———. *A Guide to Hawk Watching in North America.* University Park, PA: Penn State University Press, 1979.

———. *Guide to Owl Watching in North America.* Piscataway, NJ: Winchester Press, 1984.

———. *The Migrations of Hawks.* Bloomington, IN: Indiana University Press, 1986.

Hickey, Joseph J. (Editor). *Peregrine Falcon Populations/Their Biology and Decline.* Madison, WI: University of Wisconsin Press, 1969.

Johnsgard, Paul A. *North American Owls/Biology and Natural History.* Washington, DC: Smithsonian Institution Press, 1988.

———. *Hawks, Eagles, & Falcons of North America.* Washington, DC: Smithsonian Institution Press, 1990.

Kerlinger, Paul. *Flight Strategies of Migrating Hawks.* Chicago, IL: University of Chicago Press, 1989.

Mikkola, Heimo. *Owls of Europe.* Vermillion, SD: Buteo Books, 1983.

Newton, Ian. *Population Ecology of Raptors.* Vermillion, SD: Buteo Books, 1979.

———. *The Sparrowhawk.* Calton, England: T & AD Poyser, 1986.

———. *Birds of Prey.* Facts On File, 1990.

Palmer, Ralph S. (Ed.). *Handbook of North American Birds. Diurnal Raptors (Part 1).* Volume 4. New Haven, CT: Yale University Press, 1988.

———. *Handbook of North American Birds. Diurnal Raptors (Part 2).* Volume 5. New Haven, CT: Yale University Press, 1988.

Poole, Alan F. *Ospreys/A Natural and Unnatural History.* Cambridge University Press, 1989.

Ratcliffe, Derek. *The Peregrine Falcon.* Vermillion, SD: Buteo Books, 1980.

Stalmaster, Mark. *The Bald Eagle.* Universe Books, 1987.

Sparks, John and Tony Soper. *Owls/Their Natural & Unnatural History.* Taplinger Publishing, 1970.

Toops, Connie. *The Enchanting Owl.* Stillwater, MN: Voyageur Press, 1990.

Village, Andrew. *The Kestrel*. London: T & AD Poyser, 1990.
Walter, Lewis Wayne. *The Book of Owls*. Alfred A. Knopf, 1974.
Watson, Donald. *The Hen Harrier*. Berkhamsted, England: T & AD Poyser, 1977.

Conservation

Agee, James K. and Darryll R. Johnson (Editors). *Ecosystem Management for Parks and Wilderness*. Seattle: University of Washington Press, 1988.
Durrell, Lee. *State Of The Ark/An Atlas of Conservation In Action*. Garden City, NY: Doubleday & Co., 1986.
Grzimek, Bernhard and Michael Grzimek. *Serengeti Shall Not Die*. Ballantine Books, 1973.
Huxley, Anthony. *Green Inheritance/The World Wildlife Fund Book of Plants*. Garden City, NY: Doubleday & Co., 1985.
Myers, Norman. *The Sinking Ark/A New Look at the Problem of Disappearing Species*. Elmsford, NY: Pergamon Press, 1979.
——. *GAIA/An Atlas of Planet Management*. Garden City, NY: Doubleday & Co., 1984.
Norse, Elliott A. *Ancient Forests of the Pacific Nothwest*. Covelo, CA: Island Press, 1990.
Soulé, Michael E. and Kathryn A. Kohm. *Research Priorities For Conservation Biology*. Covelo, CA: Island Press, 1989.
Western, David and Mary Pearl. *Conservation for the Twenty-first Century*. Oxford University Press, 1989.
Whitfield, Philip, Peter D. Moore, and Barry Cox. *The Atlas of The Living World*. Boston, MA: Houghton Mifflin Co., 1989.
Yeager, Roger and Norman A. Miller. *Wildlife, Wild Death/Land Use and Survival in Eastern Africa*. Albany, NY: State University of New York Press, 1986.

Deer

Putman, Rory. *The Natural History of Deer*. Ithaca, NY: Cornell University Press, 1988.
Rue, Leonard Lee III. *The Deer of North America*. Outdoor Life Books, 1978.
Ryden, Hope. *The Little Deer of the Florida Keys*. Port Salerno, FL: Florida Classics Library, 1978.
Shissler, Bryon P. *White-tailed Deer Biology and Management in Pennsylvania*. Conestoga, PA: Wildlife Managers, 1985.

Ecotourism

Edington, John M. and M. Ann Edington. *Ecology, Recreation and Tourism*. Cambridge University Press, 1986.

Endangered Species and Extinction

Allen, Glover M. *Extinct and Vanishing Mammals of the Western Hemisphere*. Special Publication No. 11. American Committee for International Wild Life Protection, 1942.

Collar, N. J. and P. Andrew. *Birds to Watch/The ICBP World Checklist of Threatened Birds*. ICBP Technical Publication No. 8. Washington, DC: Smithsonian Institution Press, 1988.

Ehrlich, Paul and Anne Ehrlich. *Extinction*. Random House, 1981.

Fuller, Errol. *Extinct Birds*. Facts On File, 1987.

Greenway, James C., Jr. *Extinct and Vanishing Birds of the World*. Special Publication No. 13. American Committee for International Wild Life Protection, 1958.

Kaufman, Les and Kenneth Mallory. *The Last Extinction*. Cambridge, MA: MIT Press, 1986.

King, Warren B. *Endangered Birds of the World/The ICBP Bird Red Data Book*. Washington, DC: Smithsonian Institution Press, 1979.

Kohm, Kathryn A. (Editor). *Balancing On The Brink Of Extinction/The Endangered Species Act and Lessons for the Future*. Covelo, CA: Island Press, 1991.

Temple, Stanley A. *Endangered Birds/Management Techniques for Preserving Threatened Species*. Madison, WI: University of Wisconsin Press, 1978.

Whitlock, Ralph. *Birds at Risk/A Comprehensive World-Survey of Threatened Species*. Atlantic Highlands, NJ: Humanities Press, 1981.

Environmental Activism

Comp, T. Allan. *Blueprint for the Environment*. Salt Lake City, UT: Howe Brothers, 1989.

Elkington, John, Julia Hailes, and Joel Makower. *The Green Consumer*. Penguin Books, 1990.

MacEachern, Diane. *Save Our Planet/750 Everyday Ways You Can Help Clean Up The Earth*. Dell, 1990.

Furs and Leghold Trapping

Nilsson, Greta. *Facts About Furs*. Third Edition. Washington, DC: Animal Welfare Institute, 1980.

Novak, Milan et al (Editors). *Wild Furbearer Management and Conservation in North America*. Canada: Ontario Ministry of Natural Resources, 1987.

———. *Furbearer Harvests in North America, 1600–1984*. Canada: Ontario Ministry of Natural Resources, 1987.

Oceans and Marine Ecology

Bulloch, David K. *The Wasted Ocean*. Lyons & Burford, 1989.

Cousteau, Jacques. *The Living Sea*. Nick Lyons Books, 1963.

———. *The Silent World*. Nick Lyons Books, 1987.

Hoel, Michael L. *Land's Edge/A Natural History of Barrier Beaches from Maine to North Carolina*. Chester, CT: Globe Pequot Press, 1986.

Lineaweaver, Thomas H. III and Richard H. Backus. *The Natural History of Sharks*. Nick Lyons Books, 1970.

Miller, Dorcas S. *The Maine Coast/A Nature Lover's Guide*. Chester, CT: Globe Pequot Press, 1979.

Pacheco, Anthony L. and Susan E. Smith. *Marine Parks and Aquaria of the United States*. Nick Lyons Books, 1989.

Predators and Predation

Bauer, Erwin. *Predators of North America*. Outdoor Life Books, 1988.

Craighead, John J. and Frank C. Craighead, Jr. *Hawks, Owls and Wildlife*. Harrisburg, PA: Stackpole Company, 1956.

Errington, Paul L. *Of Predation and Life*. Ames, IA: Iowa State University Press, 1967.

Nichol, John. *Bites & Stings/The World of Venomous Animals*. Facts On File, 1989.

Pfeffer, Pierre. *Predators and Predation*. Facts On File, 1989.

Schueler, Donald G. *Incident At Eagle Ranch/Predators As Prey In The American West*. Tucson, AZ: University of Arizona Press, 1991.

Regional Natural History

Conrader, Jay M. and Constance Conrader. *Northwoods Wildlife Region*. Happy Camp, CA: Naturegraph Publishers, 1984.

DiNunzio, Michael G. *Adirondack Wildguide/A Natural History of the Adirondack Park*. Elizabethtown, NY: Adirondack Council, 1984.

Miller, Dorcas S. *The Maine Coast/A Nature Lover's Guide*. Chester, CT: Globe Pequot Press, 1979.

Oplinger, Carl S. and Robert Halma. *The Poconos/An Illustrated Natural History*. New Brunswick, NJ: Rutgers University Press, 1988

Tropical Forests

Bates, Henry Walter. *The Naturalist on the River Amazons*. Dover Publications, Inc., 1975.

Bunker, Stephen G. *Underdeveloping the Amazon/Extraction, Unequal Exchange, and the Failure of the Modern State*. Chicago, IL: University of Chicago Press, 1985.

Caufield, C. *In the Rainforest*. Alfred A. Knopf, 1985.

Collins, Mark (Editor). *The Last Rain Forests/A World Conservation Atlas*. Oxford University Press, 1990.

Eisenberg, John F. *Mammals of the Neotropics/The Northern Neotropics*. Volume 1. Chicago, IL: University of Chicago Press, 1989.

Emmons, Louise H. and Francois Feer. *Neotropical Rainforest Mammals/A Field Guide*. Chicago, IL: University of Chicago Press,1990.

Gradwohl, Judith and Russell Greenberg. *Saving The Tropical Forests*. Covelo, CA: Island Press, 1988.

Griffiths, Michael. *Indonesian Eden/Aceb's Rainforest*. Baton Rouge, LA: Louisiana State University Press,1990.

Huxley, Anthony. *Green Inheritance*. Garden City, NY: Anchor Press/ Doubleday, 1985.

Janzen, Daniel H. (Editor). *Costa Rican Natural History*. Chicago, IL: University of Chicago Press, 1983.

Kricher, John C. *A Neotropical Companion/An Introduction of the Animals, Plants, and Ecosystems of the New World Tropics*. Princeton, NJ: Princeton University Press, 1989.

Myers, Norman. *The Primary Source: Tropical Forests and Our Future*. W. W. Norton, 1984.

——. *GAIA/An Atlas of Planet Management*. Anchor Press/Doubleday, 1984.

Revkin, Andrew. *The Burning Season/The Murder of Chico Mendes and the Fight for the Amazon Rain Forest*. Boston, MA: Houghton Mifflin Co., 1990.

Richard, Paul W. *The Life of the Jungle*. McGraw-Hill, 1970.

Shelford, Robert W. *A Naturalist in Borneo*. Oxford University Press, 1985.

Skutch, Alexander F. *A Bird Watcher's Adventures in Tropical America*. Austin, TX: University of Texas Press, 1977.

——. *A Naturalist on a Tropical Farm*. Berkeley, CA: University of California Press, 1980.
——. *Nature through Tropical Windows*. Berkeley, CA: University of California Press, 1983.
——. *A Naturalist Amid Tropical Splendor*. Iowa City, IA, University of Iowa Press, 1987.

Whales and Dolphins

Coffey, D. J. *Dolphins, Whales and Porpoises: An Encyclopedia of Sea Mammals*. Macmillan, 1977.
Corrigan, Patricia. *Where The Whales Are/Your Guide To Whale-Watching Trips in North America*. Chester, CT: Globe Pequot Press, 1991.
Ellis, Richard. *The Book of Whales*. Alfred A. Knopf, 1980.
——. *Dolphins and Porpoises*. Alfred A. Knopf, 1982.
Hoyt, Erich. *The Whale Called Killer*. E. P. Dutton, 1981.
Katona, Steven K. et al. *Humpback Whales/A Catalogue of Individuals Identified by Fluke Photographs*. Second Edition. Bar Harbor, ME: College of the Atlantic, 1980.
Kirkevold, Barbara C. and Joan S. Lockard. *Behavioral Biology of Killer Whales*. Alan R. Liss, 1986.
Lockley, Ronald M. *Whales, Dolphins & Porpoises*. W. W. Norton & Co., Inc., 1979.
Watson, Lyall. *Sea Guide to Whales of the World*. E. P. Dutton, 1981.

Wildlife Protection

Amory, Cleveland. *Man Kind? Our Incredible War on Wildlife*. Harper & Row, 1974.
Baker, Ron. *The American Hunting Myth*. Vantage Press, 1985.
Brooks, Paul. *Speaking For Nature*. Boston, MA: Houghton Mifflin, 1980.
Collard, Andrae with Joyce Contrucci. *Rape of the Wild/Man's Violence Against Animals and the Earth*. Bloomington, IN: Indiana University Press, 1989.
Scheffer, Victor B. *A Voice For Wildlife/A Call For A New Ethic In Conservation*. Charles Scribner's Sons, 1974.

Wolves

Allen, D. L. *The Wolves of Minong: Their Vital Role In a Wild Community*. Boston, MA: Houghton Mifflin, 1979.
Harrington, F. H. and P. C. Paquet (Eds.) *Wolves of the World*. Park Ridge, NJ: Noyes Publications, 1982.

Klinghammer, E. (Ed.). *The Behavior and Ecology of Wolves*. Garland STPM Press, 1979.

Mech, L. David. *The Wolves of Isle Royale. Fauna of the National Parks of the United States*. Fauna Series 7. Washington, DC: National Park Service, 1966.

——. *The Wolf: The Ecology and Behavior of an Endangered Species*. Garden City, NY: Natural History Press, 1970.

——. *The Arctic Wolf: Living with the Pack*. Stillwater, MN: Voyageur Press, 1988.

Murie, A. *The Wolves of Mount McKinley. Fauna of the National Parks of the United States*. Fauna Series No. 5. Washington, DC: National Park Service, 1944.

Peterson, R. O. *Wolf Ecology and Prey Relationships on Isle Royale*. National Park Service Scientific Monograph Series No. 11., 1977.

Zimen, E. *The Wolf: A Species in Danger*. Delacorte, 1981.

Urban Ecology and Wildlife

Adams, Lowell W. *Integrating Man and Nature in The Metropolitan Environment*. Columbia, MD: National Institute for Urban Wildlife, 1987.

Hodge, Guy R. (Ed.). *Pocket Guide To The Humane Control of Wildlife in Cities and Towns*. Washington, DC: Humane Society of the United States, 1990.

Merilees, Bill. *Attracting Backyard Wildlife/A Guide For Nature-Lovers*. Stillwater, MN: Voyageur Press, 1989.

Moll, Gary and Sara Ebenreck. *Shading Our Cities/A Resource Guide For Urban And Community Forests*. Covelo, CA: Island Press, 1989.

INDEX

160